Mary Lean

Pollution
and the Environment

Macdonald Children's Books

Published by Macdonald Educational
Simon & Schuster International Group
Wolsey House, Wolsey Road
Hemel Hempstead HP2 4SS

First published in Great Britain by
Macdonald & Co (Publishers) Ltd 1985

Reprinted 1989

Printed in Great Britain by
BPCC Paulton Books Ltd.

British Library Cataloguing in Publication Data
Lean, Mary
   Pollution & the environment. – (Debates)
   1. Pollution
   I. Title   II.Series
   353.7'3   TD174
   ISBN 0-7500-0019-8

Contents

What is pollution?

A few decades ago no-one had climbed Mount Everest. Today its south col is littered with oxygen cylinders, axes and crampons left behind by the hundreds of mountaineers who have passed that way. The water at base camp is now too polluted to drink and expeditions have bared the mountainsides by cutting down trees for their fires.

The explorers did not set out to pollute and destroy. Everest must have seemed so remote and vast that it didn't matter what they did there. Now people like the German mountaineer Herman Warth are calling for tighter controls on expeditions.

> 'Man did not weave the web of life, he is merely a strand in it.' *Chief Seattle, 1855*

Only one Earth What has happened on Everest is a picture of what we are doing to the environment as a whole. 'The environment,' explained Einstein, 'is everything that isn't me.' It is the whole natural system on which we depend – the air we breathe, the earth which feeds us, the rivers and seas which give us water, the atmosphere around our planet which makes life possible, and all the living things which share it with us. It seems so vast that few of us give it much thought. Yet it is limited. We have only one Earth – and we may be destroying it.

Mankind is disrupting the environment in two main ways. Firstly, we are using it up – turning forests and fields into deserts and cities, destroying tens of thousands of species of wildlife and plants, guzzling natural resources of minerals and fuel so fast that w are beginning to run short. Secondly, we ar putting things into the environment whic shouldn't be there, making it a more danger ous place to live in. This book deals with th second challenge – pollution. (The first, con servation, is the subject of another book i this series.)

What do you think of when you hear th word pollution? Oil slicks at sea Factories belching out smoke? Exhaus fumes in the high street? Litter in the park Chemicals in our food? Noise? Dirt Smells? Disease? A Chinese delegate t the 1972 UN conference on the environ ment said, 'Poverty is the worst form o pollution'. Some would take the term eve further to include pornography or idea like racism which 'pollute the mind'. simple definition of pollution might b 'something in the wrong place'.

The pollution debate Pollution ranges from the annoying to the deadly, from the thing we all do most days to the concerns of bi industries. Environmentalists are ofte accused of putting the countryside befor people's need for jobs and pay; businessme of putting quick profits before the long-ter interests of humanity.

In between these two extremes there ar hard choices to be made by real people. Ca we have the comforts of modern life withou the dangers of pollution? Whether the issu is acid rain, pesticides, lead in petrol o cancer agents in food, the debate usuall comes down to three questions. How sur are experts that there is a real danger? Wha will it cost to do something about it? And is i worth it?

Opposite Pollution's most familiar face – litter in the countryside.

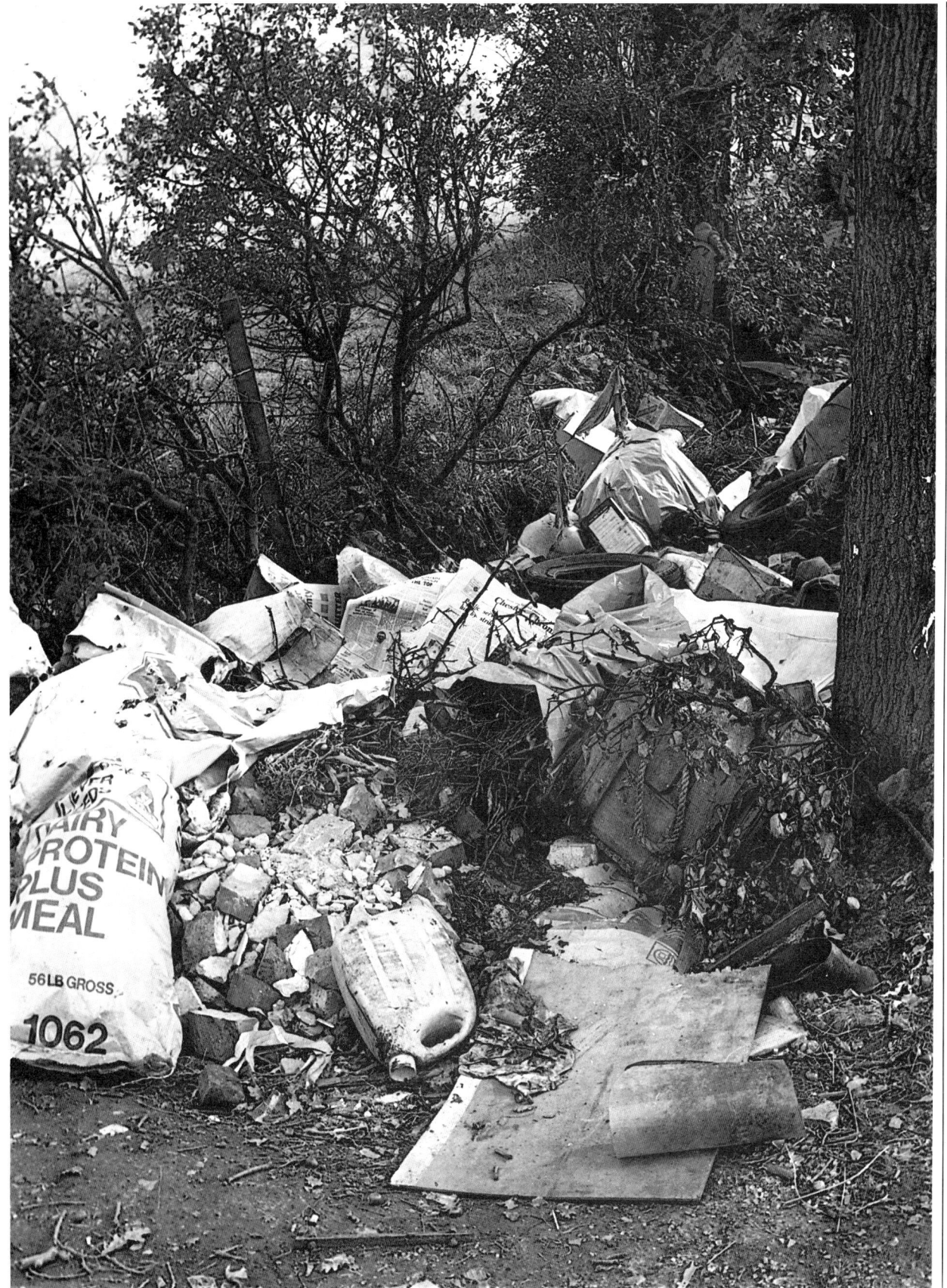

Types of

P
ollution is the nasty surprise which often follows a new discovery which could benefit mankind. The problem usually arises when we present nature with more wastes than she can cope with – or when we invent new chemicals which cannot be broken down by natural processes.

Something only becomes a pollutant when it does damage. A substance can be a lifesaver in one situation and a killer in another. Asbestos brakes and asbestos fire-proofing have undoubtedly saved thousands of lives – but thousands of workers have died because of the dust they inhaled making them. The ozone layer round the Earth shields us from the sun's lethal rays, but ozone in city air is bad for the eyes, throat and lungs.

Some pollutants work in teams – and create more problems together than they did apart. Working with asbestos and smoking cigarettes are both risky. Combined they make you ten times more likely to die of lung cancer than someone who does neither. Sulphur dioxide and smoke in the air add up to bronchial disease for city dwellers; certain mixtures of chromium and nickel pollution are ten times more dangerous to rainbow trout than you would expect from adding their separate effects together.

Sometimes, even, the teams are made up of substances which are harmless by themselves – for instance, some scientists believe that slight traces of different chemicals present in drinking water may combine to cause cancer.

Pollutants can be divided into four main categories:

Natural pollutants The world's most lethal form of pollution is untreated sewage. The World Health Organization estimates that dirty water is the reason for four-fifths of the world's disease. It kills up to 25 million people in the Third World every year.

Natural organisms break down biological wastes. Many water pollution problems are the result of our overloading this system.

Minerals Mercury, cadmium, lead, zinc and the other heavy metals are natural substances – but their chemical composition is so simple that nature cannot break them down. Now that we use heavy metals so much, this can cause problems. Because they are long-lasting they can build up in animals' bodies, becoming more concentrated as they pass up the food chain. A fish which has eaten smaller fish

may end up with 10,000 times as much mercury in its body as there is in the water around it.

Mercury is used in pesticides, in papermaking and in many other industrial processes. Mercury-poisoned fish crippled and killed hundreds of people in Japan in the '50s and '60s; mercury-contaminated bread killed 452 in Iraq in 1971-2.

Cadmium, used in metal plating and batteries, is also dangerous to people. Cadmium pollution has been caused by zinc-mining and smelting. It attacks kidneys and lungs – and can cause bones to disintegrate in what, since a fatal outbreak in 1955, the Japanese have called 'itai itai' (ouch ouch) disease.

Lead, used in petrol, paint, tin solder and in piping, is a brain poison, which is particularly dangerous to children.

Asbestos, another mineral but not a heavy metal, is also a dangerous pollutant. Fire-resistant and so fine and pliable that it can be woven and spun like cloth, it is used in building materials and brake linings.

pollution

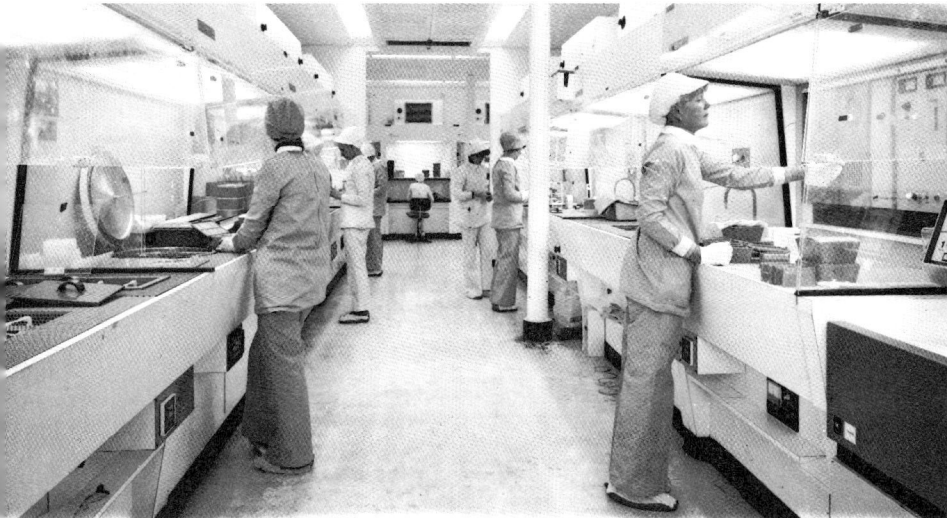

Workers in the microelectronics industry observe scrupulous standards of hygiene. But even the cleanest-looking factories can cause pollution, as people in Silicon Valley, home of California's high technology, are discovering. Poisonous chemicals have been found leaking into local water supplies. The industry may also be adding to the state's smog problems.

Asbestos dust can cause cancers and asbestosis, a fatal lung disease.

Fuels When fossil fuels – coal, gas and oil – are burned they release a number of poisonous gases which can harm people, plants and buildings. In 1952 smog in London killed 4,000 people. More recent problems include photochemical smog and acid rain. Carbon dioxide from burning fossil fuels may also be upsetting the atmospheric balance which controls our climate.

Uranium – the basic fuel for nuclear energy – causes the world's most feared pollution – radiation. Some of uranium's by-products will be lethal for thousands of years. Radiation can kill, cause cancer and birth defects, and its effects may pass down generations.

Manmade chemicals A thousand new chemicals are manufactured every year. At least 55,000 are on sale. We only know whether a fraction of them cause cancer.

Some manmade chemicals combine elements which are rarely found together in nature and therefore only break down very slowly. They can build up like the heavy metals. They include organochlorine pesticides like DDT – blamed for killing birds of prey in the '60s – and the PCB and PBB family of fire-retardant, insulating and plasticizing chemicals. In 1973 cattle in Michigan, USA, began to die after fire-retardant was mixed with their feed by mistake. 97% of the state's population were contaminated in some way by eating meat or dairy products. Many of these persistent chemicals are now restricted, but the ones which have replaced them – like the new pesticides – may cause problems of their own.

Chemical hazards reach us through the air or water, or as flavourings, preservatives or colourings in the food we eat. Hazardous chemicals are a major cause of industrial accidents or diseases, as are other dangerous substances, like asbestos or coal dust.

A Japanese city-dweller wears a mask to protect himself from pollution. Photochemical smog (see page 9) was particularly severe in Japan in the early '70s.

A new

A sandstone figure from Herten Castle, on the outskirts of West Germany's heavily industrialized Ruhr, illustrates the accelerating pace of pollution. The first photo (*below right*) shows how she looked in 1908, 206 years after she was carved. The photo on the opposite page, taken in 1969, shows how 60 years of heavy air pollution have changed her.

Did pollution finish off the Roman Empire? The Romans stored wine in lead vats and some scholars think lead poisoning weakened their minds and lay behind the fall of their civilization. High lead levels have been found in Roman skeletons. Other historians suggest that Napoleon, Ivan the Terrible and Charles II may all have died of mercury poisoning.

Air pollution has been with us since the first caveman choked in his neighbour's smoke. In 1306 Edward I banned the burning of sea-coal by London craftsmen, because it made 'so powerful and unbearable a stench'.

No sun on weekdays? Worse was to come with the Industrial Revolution. A French visitor to Manchester in 1835 wrote: 'A sort of black smoke covers the city. Under this half-daylight 300,000 human beings are ceaselessly at work.' Ten years later, Friedrich Engels had sharp things to say about the city's rivers: 'At the bottom flows, or rather stagnates, the Irk, a narrow, coal-black, foul-smelling stream.' Across the Pennines in Leeds, you could only see the sun on Sundays.

Repeated cholera epidemics in London in the nineteenth century eventually led to the first attempts at sewage control. During the early twentieth century people increasingly realized that polluted air, too, was a killer. In 1930, 6,000 people became ill because of smog in the Meuse Valley, Belgium, and 60 died. American cities like Pittsburgh, so dark that drivers sometimes had to use their headlights at midday, began to impose smoke controls in the 1930s and '40s. London followed suit after the Great Smog of 1952. Smokeless zones were enforced and industries and power stations began to build tall smokestacks to throw the pollutants to the winds. Londoners now enjoy 70% more sunshine in December than they did in 1958.

> **'The annual loss of life from filth and bad ventilation is greater than the loss in any wars.'**
> *Edwin Chadwick, social reformer, 1842*

problem ?

As old problems disappeared, new ones emerged. In 1943 people in Los Angeles became aware of a yellow-brown haze which made their eyes smart. By 1962 Los Angeles suffered from photochemical smog 212 days in the year. The problem was eventually traced to a chemical reaction between car exhaust fumes and sunlight. Photochemical smog plagues cities all over the world – only countries with dull climates, like Britain, escape. In the '70s, America and Japan moved to control vehicle fumes by fitting special converters to car exhausts.

Discovering the environment The pace of pollution quickened with the industrial boom in America, Europe and Japan after the Second World War. Japan's heavy metal tragedies in the '50s alerted people to new dangers, while Rachel Carson's book *Silent Spring*, published in 1962, painted a picture of a countryside destroyed by pesticides. By the end of the '60s the environment was in fashion – the *New York Times* carried over 1,600 articles on environmental issues in 1970, eight times as many as it had in 1960.

It was becoming clear that pollution could not be beaten by individual nations on their own. Pollutants thrown into the sea could end up on another country's shores; gases dispersed on the winds could poison another country's lakes. Some pollutants might even be affecting the Earth's atmosphere. In 1972, 113 countries met at a UN conference in Stockholm to discuss these problems – a landmark in itself. But in the 1980s, most of them still remain unresolved.

What have we done

Sweden is fighting back against acid rain by spraying lime onto affected lakes. Energy industries believe liming will buy time for more research into the causes of acid rain; Scandinavian researchers say it is 'like taking aspirin to cure cancer'.

'We have nice breezes to carry off the emissions and dissipate them.'
Governor of South Carolina

to the rain **?**

all smokestacks push sulphur dioxide and nitrogen oxides from power stations high above the lungs of city dwellers. This has solved local smog problems, but means that the pollution is blown somewhere else. Some comes down as gas relatively near home, corroding metals and buildings and damaging crops. The rest turns into acids in the atmosphere and falls as rain and fog, hundreds of miles away, poisoning lakes and forests. This 'acid rain' has caused problems in Europe and Russia, parts of Canada and the United States, and even in Brazil.

The world's most acid rain recorded fell in Pitlochry, Scotland, in 1974. It was sourer than vinegar. The average raindrop in Europe is not nearly as acid as that – but is still up to twice as acid as it was 30 years ago.

Lakes and forests Acid rain does most harm in areas like southern Sweden and Norway, where the soil is too thin and low in lime to neutralize the acid in the rainwater which falls on to it. This pours off the land into the lakes and rivers, setting off a chain reaction which kills most life. The Swedes say 22,000 of their lakes are sick and fish have died out in lakes and rivers in Scandinavia, Canada, the United States and Scotland.

In other areas, many scientists believe acid rain is part of a witch's brew of pollutants which is killing the forests. West Germany says that half of hers are dying – and millions of acres are affected all over Europe and in North America.

Whose responsibility? The acid rain debate today centres on who should do what about it. The Swedes spend millions of pounds a year liming their lakes to make them less acid. A Swedish Ministry of Agriculture report in 1982 insisted that this is no permanent solution – the problem must be solved at its source, in the power stations abroad from which 70% of their sulphur pollution comes.

The technology exists to halve Western Europe's sulphur dioxide and nitrous oxide emissions by the year 2010 – but it could add at least 5% to electricity prices to do so. This makes countries such as Britain, Europe's largest acid rain exporter in the early '80s, cautious. Since everyone needs electricity, the expense would 'lower everyone's standard of living', according to the Chairman of Britain's Central Electricity Generating Board, Sir Walter Marshall, in 1983. 'It would be tragic to do this without understanding exactly what we are doing.'

Sceptics point out that the science of acid rain is complicated. Why penalize power stations until we are sure they are the culprits? There is no doubt, for example, that some of the trouble is caused by car exhausts. They also release sulphur dioxide and are the main source of nitrogen oxide and ozone pollution. Many scientists believe cars, not power stations, are the real killers of the German forests.

Meanwhile, America's largest electrical power system, the Tennessee Valley Authority, has already halved its sulphur dioxide emissions. 'Concern about bills and job prospects are very real,' says its Director, David Freeman. 'But they must give way to concern over life itself. The typical consumer is now paying $4 on each bill for cleaner air.'

Is acid rain, as *Nature* magazine once put it, 'a million dollar problem with a billion dollar solution'? The importing countries see things differently. 'The Black Forest is beyond price,' said the Prime Minister of Baden Wurttemburg, West Germany, in 1983. 'We cannot wait for a perfect understanding of the acid rain phenomenon before moving to control it,' commented a Canadian official in February 1981. 'How many more lakes have got to die before we get the message?'

Changing

The world's climate is like a giant seesaw, wrote the environmentalist Barbara Ward – the slightest shift can unbalance it. A change in the earth's temperature of only 1 or 2 degrees Centigrade, either way, could completely alter the world – and some believe this might happen within our lifetimes.

Natural events can shift this balance – like the eruption of Mount St Helens, which has been blamed for the cool summer of 1980. But what about man's activities? Scientists, farmers, governments and energy suppliers are locked in debate about this.

Hotting up or cooling down? Man's main impact on the climate is probably through burning fossil fuels – coal, oil and gas – which release carbon dioxide (CO_2) into the atmosphere. The CO_2 around the earth acts a bit like the glass around a greenhouse – it lets the sun's heat in, but not out. So more CO_2 in the atmosphere could make the earth warmer.

A small group of scientists, led by the American Reid Bryson, believe the opposite – that pollution is cooling the earth down. When a volcano erupts, it sends clouds of dust into the atmosphere, which act as a sunshield. Bryson thinks the dust thrown up by power stations and factories and blown off farmland acts in the same way, blocking out the warmth of the sun. But this is not generally causing as much concern as the so-called 'greenhouse effect'.

A warmer, hungrier world? The debate is based on what one scientist called a 'pyramid of uncertainty'. How much CO_2 will be released in the next 50 years? How much will the oceans absorb? Is deforestation making things worse? What about other 'greenhouse gases' – whose combined effect is now thought to be as serious as CO_2? Will the pollution really make the earth warmer?

Not even the most sophisticated computers can tell us for sure. But most scientists agree that we could add up to 4.5 degrees Centigrade to the earth's temperature by the middle of the next century. This could drastically rearrange the world's climate, to which mankind is 'finely tuned'. The world's best grainlands could move northwards from the USA to Canada and Siberia. A hungry world

'It is probably wiser not to act aggressively to solve the problem now, when we do not know the consequences.'

US National Academy of Sciences, 1983

the climate ?

might run even more short of food before we have time to adapt. As the oceans become warmer, their upper waters could expand, raising sea-level and flooding farmland and cities all over the world. The melting of glaciers could add to this effect.

What should be done? Two US 1983 reports disagreed – one, by the National Academy of Sciences, advised 'concern, not panic'; the other, by the Environmental Protection Agency, warned that the greenhouse effect could begin in the 1990s and called for 'a sense of urgency'.

In 1985 international experts meeting in Villach, Austria, agreed that some warming of the climate was now inevitable. As well as taking preventative measures, they advised, countries must begin to work out how to adapt to a warmer world. 'Humanity has unwittingly embarked upon a dangerous experiment on a planetary scale,' comments environmentalist Erik Eckholm.

> 'It is undoubtedly the largest outstanding environmental problem confronting the world.'
> Holdgate, Kassas and White, The World Environment 1972-82

North America's grain surplus is 'the world's insurance against famine', says climate writer John Gribbin. In times of scarcity, Russia and the Third World rely on the vast cornlands of Canada and the USA. If global warming reduces their yield, will people starve while the world adjusts?

The ozone layer –

A vast natural filter in the stratosphere, several miles above our heads, protects us from the dangerous ultraviolet rays of the sun. This ozone layer is fragile – and environmentalists are afraid that pollution may be weakening it. Ultraviolet light can cause eye disease and skin cancers, as well as stunting plants and marine life, so the prospect is frightening.

Planes, sprays and fridges The fate of the ozone layer was one of the major environmental scares of the '70s. Fears focused first on supersonic flights, which some scientists thought would fill the stratosphere with gases which would destroy the ozone. This concern lost momentum during the decade – particularly when it turned out that there

be about to destroy his planet,' commented *The Times*. By 1981 America, Canada, Sweden and Norway had banned CFCs in all or most aerosols and the EEC and Japan had imposed limits on production. In other areas, including eastern Europe, India and Argentina, it has gone on climbing.

In spite of the heated debate, cutting CFCs in aerosols is relatively easy, as other chemicals can be used instead. But CFCs are also used in refrigerators, air-conditioners, fire-extinguishers and in making plastic foam containers for fast-food restaurants. So, in spite of the controls, world CFC production is still spiralling. Meanwhile other gases have come under suspicion – including carbon tetrachloride, methylchloroform and nitrous oxides.

When the first Concordes were being built in 1971, an American professor suggested that their exhaust fumes might damage the ozone layer. Environmentalists argued about how many aircraft would be needed to cause serious trouble – and when early estimates proved to be exaggerated, their attention switched to aerosols.

would not be many commercial supersonic airliners in the immediate future anyway.

In 1974 aerosols took over as ozone enemy number one. Experts feared that the chlorofluorocarbons (know as 'CFCs') which propel hairsprays, flykillers or airfresheners out of their cans would float slowly up to the ozone layer and remain there for decades, eating it away. 'For the price of convenience man may

Ozone hole Atmospheric chemistry still remains something of a mystery to mankind. There may, for example, be substances in the atmosphere that soak up the ozone-destroyers, while other gases – like CO_2 – may indirectly increase ozone. The CFCs released today could take 40 years to reach the ozone layer – and so, if we wait until we are absolutely sure what is happening, it may be too late to do anything about it.

Because of the uncertainties, the debate waned in the early '80s. Then, in 1984, scientists discovered a 'hole' in the ozone layer over Antarctica which appeared every spring. Swiss scientists think the same thing

'Fluorocarbons are unlikely to have a significant effect on the Earth's ozone layer.'
Dr Arthur Jones, US scientist, 1975

at risk ?

may be happening over the Arctic. Is pollution to blame? Even if the holes have natural causes, there is growing agreement that pollution is behind a less dramatic thinning of the ozone layer worldwide. In 1986, American scientists announced millions more skin cancers in the USA in the next 90 years unless CFC emissions were cut. Meanwhile it had become clear that CFCs were also adding to the greenhouse effect.

As the ozone layer cannot be divided up, only united action can protect it. In March 1985, an international agreement to protect the ozone layer was signed in Vienna under UN auspices. Two years later signatories were still arguing about how to put it into force. 'If we cannot succeed in protecting the environment in this easy way,' says Swedish scientist Bert Bolin, 'there is not much hope for the future.'

The Earth seen from space. The ozone in the atmosphere around our planet is essential to life. Are we destroying it?

Nuclear energy –

'**E**very pound of coal we can save will be less acid rain and less ozone depletion,' says Volker Mohnen, of the US Atmospheric Research Centre. Oil and gas, the cleaner fossil fuels, are running out. So where should we look for tomorrow's energy?

The ideal energy source? Energy industries and governments in most industrialized countries believe the answer to future energy needs lies in nuclear fission. This can release enough energy from a kilogram of uranium to heat a small electric fire for five and a half years. (A kilogram of coal can only keep it going for a couple of hours.)

Supporters of nuclear power claim that it is economic, much cleaner than fossil fuels, and given reasonable precautions not particularly dangerous. The next step, they say, is the fast breeder reactor which, by converting the kilogram of uranium to plutonium, will stretch its fire-heating power to over 300 years.

The anti-nuclear lobby disagrees. From the moment uranium is mined, they say, it is a threat to workers and the public. How much radiation leaks out of nuclear power stations? Is the high incidence of leukaemia among children living near some nuclear plants a coincidence? What about accidents, like the one at Chernobyl in 1986 – whose effects were felt as far away as Ireland? Is it right to create wastes which will be toxic for millennia? Fast breeders, they believe, will only increase the dangers. Plutonium is the raw material of nuclear bombs. What if terrorists get hold of it? And can governments be trusted only to use it for peace?

Hope or has-been? The heyday of nuclear planning was in the '60s and early '70s. In early days enthusiasts promised electricity 'too cheap to meter'. With the oil crisis and recession, and the soaring expense of building nuclear plants, such predictions have fallen on hard times. When the Conservative government came to power in Britain in 1979, it announced it would build a new nuclear power station every year for a decade. Eight years later, work on the first still had not begun.

American projections of nuclear capacity in 2001 dropped over 80% between 1972 and 1980. 'Nuclear power which 10 years ago was the hope of all energy planners is now a "has-been",' commented the Deputy Secretary of the US Department of Energy in 1978. Meanwhile public opinion was taking its toll – an Austrian referendum in 1978 decided to mothball a large nuclear plant, while in 1980 the Swedes voted to phase out their programme. Chernobyl reinforced these trends.

In 1986, 366 nuclear reactors were at work in 26 countries, providing 65% of France's electricity, 42% of Sweden's, 23% of Japan's, 16% of the USA's and 10% of Russia's. India expects to get 10% of her electricity from nuclear power in the '90s, while Denmark and Australia have decided not to develop nuclear power at all.

Does nuclear power hold the key to the future, or is it on the way out? Should we go for a middle road, accepting a reasonable number of today's reactors, but refusing to run the added risks of fast breeders?

'Nobody should rely for something as basic as energy on a product that produces in quantity a by-product as dangerous as plutonium, unless he is absolutely convinced there is no reasonable alternative,' stated Sir Brian Flowers, Chairman of Britain's Royal Commission on Environmental Pollution, in 1976. Do such alternatives exist?

> '*Man has not grown up enough to be trusted with nuclear reactors.*'
> Sir George Porter, winner of the Nobel Prize for chemistry

a safe alternative ?

Power

Sun, wind, rivers, sea, plants and trees, the heat inside the earth, even rubbish, could all provide 'alternative' sources of energy for mankind. Some of them cause little pollution and most have the added advantage of being renewable – the coal we burn today is gone for ever, but the wind continues to blow whether we use it or not.

But are they practical? 'In the search for new ways of making energy, there is only a thin line between science fiction and reality,' writes John Maddox, one of the sceptics.

> **'At best [conservation] means we will run out of energy a little more slowly.'**
> Ronald Reagan, before becoming US President

Tomorrow's energy today? Mankind already uses many of these energy sources. Half the world uses wood, crop wastes or dung for fuel. In 1980, according to one estimate, wood provided more of the USA's primary energy than nuclear power. Falling water provides 23% of the world's electricity. A quarter of Brazil's new cars run on alcohol fermented from plants, half of Israel's homes warm their water with the sun, and three-quarters of Iceland's heating comes from the earth. Millions of Chinese use manure to make gas and fertilizer, and

Munich in West Germany gets 12% of its electricity from burning its rubbish.

Such projects only provide a minute part of the world's energy, but many countries are looking into large-scale uses. All entail problems. Over a billion people in the Third World are running short of firewood as more trees are cut down than are replanted. Wood and geothermal power can cause pollution, as can the manufacture of solar cells. Massive windmills or hydroelectric schemes would spoil the countryside. There are money problems, geographical problems – industries might have to move to remote sites – and storage problems – what happens on a windless night? Critics believe these objections are decisive, while enthusiasts think they could be overcome if governments took them as seriously as they take nuclear power.

Can we save it? Another approach is simply to use less energy. The oil crisis has spurred most governments to set up conservation targets and even Britain, which has lagged behind the rest of Europe, now says that she could save £20 million a day by using energy more efficiently.

Energy efficiency involves insulating buildings to keep the heat in, harnessing waste heat from power stations, designing cars to run on less fuel, and personal actions like switching off lights, turning down the thermostat, or travelling by bus or train rather than by car. An Earth Resources Research study describes efficiency as 'a huge reservoir of cheap energy, larger than the North Sea oil and gas fields put together, and much more permanent'.

Washington's Worldwatch Institute believes that, with conservation, renewable resources could provide a quarter of the world's energy by the year 2000. 'Given the failed promise of nuclear power and the fact that fossil fuels are fading rapidly, major reliance on renewable energy after the year

Mankind has been harnessing the power of the wind for thousands of years – some say since 2000 BC. By the fourteenth century, the date of this illustration, windmills were common in Europe. In the nineteenth century there were 10,000 windmills at work in the Netherlands alone. The California Energy Commission aims to have windpower producing 8% of the state's energy by the year 2000.

without pollution?

000 may be essential,' says their 1984 *State of the World* report. Meanwhile most governments are planning to increase their use of alternative energy sources, but none are pinning all their hopes on them.

'Solar energy can put hundreds of thousands of Americans to work.' *Jimmy Carter, US President, 1979*

Solar One Power Station in California uses the sun to generate electricity. Hundreds of mirrors focus sunlight onto the power tower, heating its boiler to produce steam to power the turbines.

A sink for all

our wastes ?

For centuries the oceans, seas and rivers have offered mankind water, food, a highway – and an efficient waste disposal system. As rivers and seas bear our wastes away, the water bacteria break most of them down into salts, which fertilize the algae on which water creatures feed. Sunlight and salt help the sea fight harmful micro-organisms. Many scientists believe that, given skilful engineering, the sea is still the world's best sewage treatment scheme.

Overload? As cities and industries mushroomed around the world humanity began to overload this system – and to present it with chemicals and heavy metals which it could not destroy. Rivers, lakes and coastal waters, and land-locked seas like the Mediterranean, Baltic and the Persian Gulf, are all showing the strain.

There are several ways in which the natural waste disposal system can break down. Sometimes we simply give the river and sea bacteria more wastes than they can digest. As they struggle to cope, they use up more than their share of oxygen – and fish and other creatures suffocate. Both untreated sewage and industrial wastes can have this effect. Colombian scientists say that 250 km of their country's mighty Magdalena River could be entirely without oxygen by the year 2000. All the rivers around Japan's paper-making town Fuiji were short of oxygen in the early '70s.

We can also cause problems by overfertilizing the algae which grow in surface waters. The effluents from sewage farms and the run-off from farmlands are rich in the salts on which algae thrive. As more and more algae grow, they block out the light from the waters below and the plants that grow there put less oxygen into the water. When the algae die, the bacteria in the water need extra oxygen to cope with the decaying mass. In time new bacteria which need less oxygen take over

and poison the waters. In the early '70s, Lake Erie was thought to be dying of this 'overenrichment', and today the Baltic Sea and Lake Geneva are seriously ill.

We subject our waters to hundreds of stresses and strains. Waste water from power stations overheats them, disrupting the life cycle of fish. Chemicals and toxic metals poison them and the people who eat their shellfish, such as the 2,000 Japanese crippled and 400 killed by mercury pollution in Minamata Bay and Niigata. Acids and pesticides are carried to them on the winds; oil pours in from industry and ships; there is a constant risk of accidents, like the one at a Swiss chemical firm in 1986, which devastated the ecology of the Rhine.

All this can add up to disaster – lakes like Russia's Ladoga, the largest in Europe, which is being poisoned by industry; rivers like Britain's Mersey, 'the open sewer of the north-west'; seas like the Baltic, 'an alarm clock of pollution for the whole world'; beauty-spots like America's 'queen of estuaries', Chesapeake Bay, whose ecology may be fundamentally changed.

Signs of hope? At the same time there are encouraging signs. Fish have returned to waters in the USA and Britain where they haven't been seen for a century or more, lakes in Sweden and the USA have recovered from overenrichment. Nations are beginning to get together to see what they can do about the polluted rivers and seas they share.

We cannot live without creating wastes – yet dirty water is one of the world's greatest killers. How, then, can we get rid of our rubbish without destroying our environment?

Opposite The wild beauty of Kenya's Rift Valley is scarred by detergent pollution. The foam is caused by 'hard' detergents which do not degrade easily and can reduce oxygen levels and poison fish. Hard detergents are now rarely used in the developed world outside industry.

'Water, water everywhere, nor any drop to drink.'
S. T. Coleridge, The Ancient Mariner

Water

Most of the 500 families of Guruvarajapalayam, a village in South India, have lost a baby because of the world's deadliest pollutant – untreated human waste. Water-related diseases claim 25 million lives in the Third World every year, half of them small children. They kill three toddlers in India every minute and cost the country 73 million working days a year and $600 million in medical care and lost production.

> 'Nations are caught on the horns of a dilemma. How much can they squeeze other sectors during these hard times?' *World Bank official*

Over half the people in the Third World have no safe drinking water and three-quarters have no form of sanitation at all. Infections spread in crowded slums and in villages where the only toilet is the fields and where water is too precious to use for washing. In remote villages women have to trek miles every day to fetch water.

A question of money? In 1980 the UN launched the International Drinking Water Supply and Sanitation Decade. The idea was to encourage governments in the Third World to bring water, sanitation and basic hygiene education to all their people by 1990, with the help of aid from the rich countries. Even on the most basic level, this would cost the world some $80 million for each day of the decade.

Well into the decade the question is still, 'Who's going to pay?' The cost seems low compared to the $1,400 million a day the world spends on arms – or the $240 million we spend on cigarettes. But it comes at a time when rich nations are cutting back on aid. The Third World is enthusiastic about the decade as long as it means new aid from the West, rather than a diversion of aid from other development projects. Just maintaining the pumps needed to bring water to all Tanzania's villagers would cost twice the annual budget of the ministry concerned.

> 'The number of water taps per 1,000 persons is a better indication of health than the number of hospital beds.'
> *Dr Halfdan Mahler, World Health Organization*

for all?

A red herring? Water and sanitation programmes encounter problems in the villages too. The women of Guruvarajapalayam want a better water supply – but not as much as they want well-built homes and more food for their hungry families. To them, sanitation seems an unnecessary luxury. At the same time, most projects depend on local maintenance: researchers found, for example, that villagers did not always add chlorine, which kills dangerous bacteria, to their wells, partly because it was not always available and partly because they disliked its taste.

So is the decade a damp squib? No-one believes it will achieve its targets. Most Third World countries think the 'pollution of poverty' will only be ended when world economics are reformed so that they can earn enough to look after their peoples' basic needs. Is the decade a red herring? Or is it a chance of awakening the world to the needs of its poorest inhabitants?

Clean water and sanitation alone cannot save the babies of Guruvarajapalayam. But if these are not provided, they will always be in danger.

Water is available in this Calcutta shanty-town – but is it clean? Sewage seeps into the city's public water supply through cracks in the system of pipes.

Saving our

'The Mediterranean is sick. If measures are not taken promptly its illness may become incurable.'

UN Environment Programme

rivers and seas

The world's coastal and inland waters provide two of the pollution success stories of the last decade. With the slogan 'pollution is the unifying concept', the United Nations Environment Programme (UNEP) brought together ten groups of nations to clean up their shared regional seas, and other or - ganizations have sponsored agreements to protect the Red Sea, Baltic and the north-east Atlantic and Arctic. Meanwhile Britain can now boast that the Thames is the world's cleanest metropolitan estuary, with 101 kinds of fish found there compared with only one in 1963.

Do these successes mean that mankind is winning the battle against water pollution? They may mean we are beginning to. But environmentalists are quick to point out that many problems remain.

Will the plans work? Many of the advances are still only on paper. Most of UNEP's region-al seas programmes are still in the early, relatively easy, stage of general agreements and research. The pilot Mediterranean Action Plan hit difficulties, however, when it came to cutting the discharges from land which make up four-fifths of the sea's pollu-tion. It took four years to reach agreement on this and the cost will run to billions. Will states be ready to pay and to limit their industries? This will be the test of the other plans too. The programmes have brought together old enemies, like Israel and Syria, America and Cuba; but how will they work together under pressure?

Ten industrialized nations passed major water pollution laws in the 1970s. But laws cannot create clean rivers without the will and the cash to back them up. Only a quarter of the water clauses of a British act passed in 1974 were in effect in early 1984. In 1981 the National Water Council reported a cut in serious river pollution in England and Wales, but warned that in the present financial cli-mate prospects for further improvements were 'bleak'. Forced to choose priorities, many countries are adapting standards to water use – how clean, for instance, does a boating lake need to be?

Can we afford the cure? As old problems disappear, new ones emerge. A 1979 report on the industrialized countries found that less raw sewage was reaching the rivers, but more poisonous chemicals and metals. American biologists think these are giving fish cancer. Effluents from factories and sew-age plants are coming under control, but the polluted water which runs off fields and city streets and dumps is harder to check. Acid rain kills lakes in Canada and Scandinavia, and in many countries there are fears of poisons reaching underground water reserves.

In 1979 a French marine scientist de-scribed Mediterranean pollution as 'a diagnosed illness that we are in the process of treating'. The same could be said of many of the rich world's rivers and seas. Will we be able to afford to keep up the treatment? Will we want to if it means industries have to put up their prices? And what about the still undiagnosed waters of the Third World?

Opposite Bathers in the Mediterranean, it is said, run a one-in-seven risk of disease. Land-locked seas are particularly vulnerable to pollution because the water in them changes so slowly. It takes the Mediterranean 80 years to flush out its pollution. Now the nations on its shores are beginning to tackle the problem together.

Salmon returned to the River Thames in the 1970s after 140 years. Here the first angler to hook one brandishes his prize.

Do oil spills

Most Europeans think oil spills are the most worrying threat to the environment today, an EEC opinion survey found in 1984. This is not a view shared by many environmentalists.

For 11 years the wreck of the *Torrey Canyon* off Cornwall held the world oil spill record with a 'black tide' of some 100,000 tonnes. Then, in March 1978, the *Amoco Cadiz* went aground off Brittany, spilling 220,000 tonnes and killing some third of the local fauna. By mid-1980 a blow-out at the Ixtoc I oil well in the Gulf of Mexico had more than doubled the record again.

their tanks on their way home to the refineries and empty out oily ballast water. The Gulf and the Caribbean, two of the world's busiest oil routes, are particularly vulnerable. Two-thirds of the oil in the sea comes from refineries, factories and cities on land. The Mediterranean, in surface one hundredth of the world's oceans, carries half the world's floating oil and tar.

Experts disagree about how serious this chronic pollution is. Soviet scientists believe it is destroying the fisheries of the Black and Azov seas; but a British report in 1981 concluded that 'the threat of long-term, irrever-

> **'All 500 fishermen in this village are ruined for years to come. No whiting, bass or shellfish could live under that mess.'**
> Pierre Lemoine, local councillor, after Amoco Cadiz disaster, 1978

Even a small oil slick can be disastrous for flocks of seabirds in its path. It only took a 400-tonne spill to kill over 35,000 birds off Denmark in 1979. Fish, shellfish and the minute organisms they eat are also affected, with serious results for local people. Thousands of Nigerian fishermen temporarily lost their livelihood after an explosion on a Texaco rig in 1980, oyster beds were closed for 10 years after a spill in Massachusetts in 1969, and oily beaches are no help to tourism.

But the surprise recently has been how quickly sea and beach species can recover after the shock. A UN report on the health of the oceans in 1982 commented, 'Significant effects on the ecosystem have not been detected.'

Chronic pollution Only a tiny fraction of the seas' oil pollution comes from the disasters which catch the headlines. Tankers cause five times more pollution when they wash out

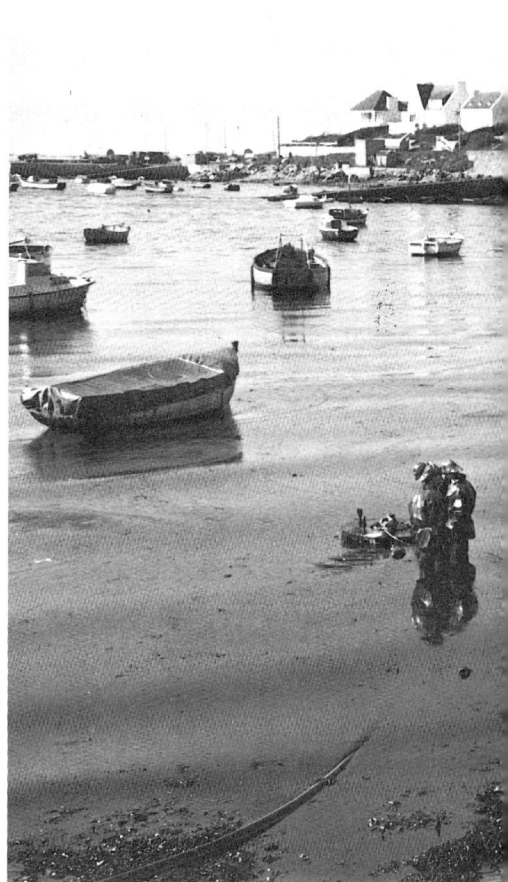

matter?

sible damage to the marine environment by oil pollution is insubstantial'.

A dangerous cure? How to clean up is another controversial question. The detergents used after the *Torrey Canyon* spill did more damage than the oil itself. Scientists have since developed new 'non-toxic' dispersants, but many countries are reluctant to use them. 'With the oil it will take four or five years to recover; with the detergent it will be 10,' warned a French marine biologist after the *Amoco Cadiz* wreck. No really effective chemical or machine for cleaning up has yet been developed.

Prevention is also difficult. The International Maritime Organization, which is responsible for this, has to wait for governments to ratify its rules – and this has led to long delays. Oil-dumpers are hard to catch, although aerial surveillance schemes planned by France and the US could help. Meanwhile a 1980 report claimed that EEC nations were inadequately prepared for accidents. A British civil servant complained in 1978 that there was so little will for reform when things were going well that 'sometimes I get down and pray for a disaster'.

Cleaning up the shore near Portsall after the *Amoco Cadiz* disaster, which killed 30% of local fish, shellfish, birds and marine animals. 'It's always the fishermen who pay,' complained a local lobster catcher. But the fishermen were back at work within six weeks.

Wastes – a drop

A way from the coasts, the oceans which cover three-quarters of our planet give few signs of being affected by pollution. Some scientists believe they are the ideal place to put the really dangerous wastes that nobody wants buried near their home. Environmental groups like Greenpeace disagree.

The debate is most heated when it comes to nuclear wastes. These are generally divided into three types – low level, which has already been dumped at sea, and intermediate and high level, which countries are storing until they know what to do with them. Some of the high-level wastes will be danger-ous for thousands of years. The chemical industry also produces rubbish which can kill or cause disease – and some of this will remain poisonous for ever. Could we solve our problems, as some nuclear scientists suggest, by burying them at sea?

Do the oceans need protection? All life on earth started in the oceans and they still tune our climate and give us oxygen and rain. They also have a vast capacity for watering down our wastes. 'Some quantity of any material, no matter how noxious its qualities, can be introduced into the sea without pro-

Seamen spray water on Greenpeace demonstrators who are trying to stop them from dumping drums of low-level nuclear waste into the north-east Atlantic.

'The ocean's capacity to degrade and disperse waste materials is under-utilized.'
Alan Preston, UK Fisheries Laboratory

in the ocean ?

ducing unacceptable effects,' says marine scientist Alan Preston. He believes that disasters like the mercury poisoning at Minamata in Japan (see page 21) have led to 'overprotection' of the sea, sometimes at the cost of the land.

Environmentalists like the explorer Thor Heyerdahl disagree. 'When you step onto a few logs on one continent and drift to the other side, you realize how small and vulnerable the ocean is,' he says. 'Man today overestimates the size of the oceans and underestimates their importance for life on this planet.' Like many other parts of our life-support system, we may only notice that things are going wrong in the oceans when it is too late.

When the dumping had to stop The nuclear dumping debate came to a head in the early 1980s at meetings of the London Dumping Convention, the international body which regulates waste disposal from ships. In 1983, its signatories decided to halt the dumping of low-level wastes to give time for research. Some countries tried to ignore this resolution, but by September 1983 a trade union boycott had forced even Britain, the world's biggest nuclear dumper at sea, to give way.

Meanwhile pressure built up to stop France and Britain pumping liquid wastes directly into the sea from their reprocessing plants at Cap de la Hague and Windscale (Sellafield). In 1984 Britain agreed to cut these discharges almost entirely.

The USA, France, Germany, Britain, Japan and the Netherlands want research into burying high-level wastes deep under the ocean bed. Other countries are against even considering this. Putting the most lethal wastes under the ocean bed has the advantage of putting them as far away from people as possible, but the disadvantage that we can't keep an eye on them. The low-level wastes – including rubbish from hospitals and laboratories as well as from the nuclear industry – may not be particularly harmful if they are dumped in the sea in containers, although liquid wastes from reprocessing plants have caused serious concern.

The nuclear wastes debate is really about the future of nuclear energy itself. If we want nuclear power, we will have to find somewhere to put the wastes. 'If the nuclear industry is forced to land-store low-level waste, the continued growth of the nuclear power programme will be put in jeopardy,' says Greenpeace.

'If the cradle of life is shattered, what happens to life?

Barbara Ward, environmentalist

Buried

At Love Canal, near Niagara Falls in the USA, basements began to smell of chemicals and children came home with holes burnt in their shoes. In Lekkerkerk, Holland, poisons got into the water supply. Both estates had been built on forgotten chemical waste dumps – and had to be evacuated. In Toyama, Japan, rice grown on land polluted by zinc-mining wastes killed 100 people; in Missouri authorities are still cleaning up after an illegal dumper who sprayed herbicide wastes on stableyards and roadsides 13 years ago; and 11 people were poisoned when insecticide, buried 40 years earlier, polluted a well in Perham, Minnesota.

are ticking timebombs all over,' warned Stefan Plehn of the US Environmental Protection Agency in 1978. 'We just don't know how many Love Canals there are.'

Some wastes can be burnt, some treated or solidified before disposal, some put into open pits or spread on land, some buried. Each country has its favourite method – the USA concentrates on leak-proof sites; Britain believes in 'dilute and disperse'; Germany uses old salt-mines for its most dangerous rubbish; in 1984 Irish firms still had to treat their own waste or export it; the Dutch cannot bury much of theirs because their water supplies are so near the surface.

> **'Toxic chemical waste may be the sleeping giant of this decade.'**
> *Former US Congressman John E. Moss*

The USA produces some 60 million tonnes of hazardous wastes a year; the EEC about 25 million. They may be poisonous, corrosive, explosive or long-lasting and, wrongly disposed of, they can cause terrible problems. As some wastes are harmless until they are combined with others, and many are produced in small quantities and mixed with innocent substances, they can be hard to keep track of. 'We do not know how much hazardous waste is produced in the UK, who produces it, what it is nor what happens to it,' says Britain's main hazardous waste research centre at Harwell.

How many Love Canals? Disasters like the one at Love Canal in the States have led to strict legislation. The USA, Netherlands and West Germany have the tightest controls, requiring firms that create, transport or dispose of hazardous wastes to be licensed. But even iron rules can do nothing about the problems left by an easy-going past. 'There

dangers ?

Chemical dustbins? As countries tighten their controls, will more lenient nations become hazardous dustbins? When Holland clamped down after Lekkerkerk, one company began to export its wastes to Britain. The USA exports large quantities of wastes to Britain and Japan. The EEC agreed strict cross-frontier transport rules after drums of poisonous dioxin from Italy turned up in a French slaughterhouse in 1983. Meanwhile there are fears that companies may use Third World countries as chemical dumping grounds.

Everyone wants hazardous wastes to be disposed of safely – but preferably not near them. As governments and industry try to decide what to do, environmentalists take the argument a stage further back. How many of these wastes do we need to create in the first place?

> 'You could have told me it was some kind of a new jelly and I'd have put it on toast and eaten it.'
>
> Russell Bliss, who sprayed dioxin along Missouri roadsides, 1971

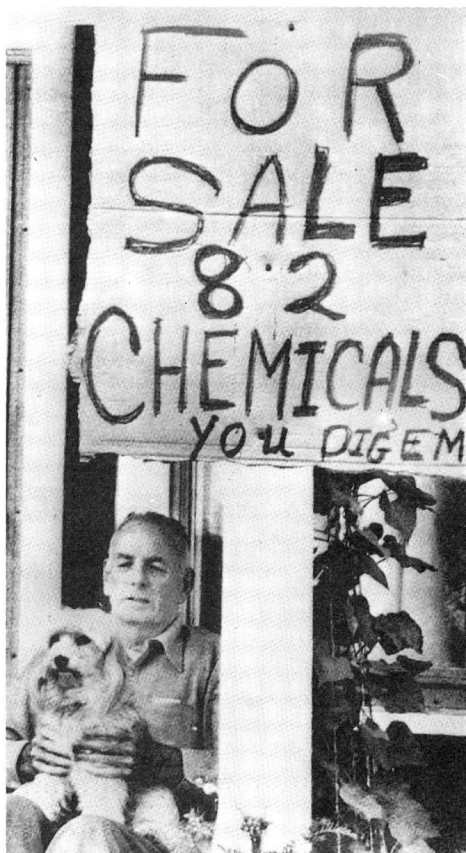

Far left A fire at Pitsea, Britain's largest waste tip, in 1978. Britain's answer to the problem of hazardous waste is to mix it with domestic rubbish, which filters and dilutes the poisons. 'How much poison can a gigantic sponge like Pitsea take before it is saturated?' ask critics.

Left A Love Canal resident's wry response to the discovery that he was living on a forgotten chemical waste dump.

Can we afford

E very year Americans on average throw away nearly a tonne of rubbish each, and you could build 60 Egyptian pyramids out of the contents of Britain's dustbins. Environmentalists believe we could learn something from the cities of the Third World where, according to Oxfam, 'every tin can, every motor tyre and every scrap of paper is collected for recycling or reuse'.

Rubbish dumps can be a treasure trove for resourceful city councils. Waste paper, metal and glass can all be reprocessed. Kitchen leftovers can be turned into compost. Other wastes can be converted into fuel. Machida, Japan's 'garbage capital', now recycles 90% of its rubbish. Industries are finding they can recycle their polluting wastes – or use them to make lucrative new products. Sweden helps companies to find buyers who can use their hazardous wastes, and there is a flourishing international trade in less harmful recyclables. For instance, Japan imports scrap metal from America and turns last year's Buick into next year's Toyota.

The battle of the bottles In the late 1970s EEC families threw out 9 million tonnes of drink cans and bottles a year – a mountain of litter which took over a million tonnes of oil to produce. Environmentalists want governments to ban non-returnable drinks containers and enforce a deposit and return system. Nine American states and four European countries have done this. States like Oregon, America's bottle bill pioneer, boast a high rate of returns, a 35-40% drop in litter, and more new jobs in handling bottles for refilling than were lost in bottle-making.

Bottle manufacturers elsewhere are sceptical about these figures. The system would threaten their industry and they say customers and shops would find it too much hassle. In many countries, glassmakers have come up with a compromise, setting up

Where do cars go when they die? Norway's answer to the problem is to make car-buyers pay a deposit which they get back with a bonus when they leave the car's hulk at a recovery centre.

to recycle ?

bottle banks to collect old bottles for melting down and re-making. This uses less energy than making new bottles from scratch – but much more than cleaning and refilling old ones, so some environmentalists disapprove of it. Steven Shelley of the Glass Manufacturers' Federation described Britain's scheme, set up in 1977, as 'a way of responding to environmental and consumer pressure without compromising our interests'. It has proved so successful that it seems the manufacturers have won the day. The Netherlands and Switzerland now recycle nearly half their glass.

Paper problems Recycling's success depends on markets for its products. In 1974, for example, Britain and France both found themselves with tonnes of wastepaper which the paper mills did not want. As a result some countries are using subsidies to create a steady market. Quality can also be a problem

– for the higher the grade of recycled paper produced, the more pollution involved. Can we make do with coarser toilet paper or greyer books for the sake of our rivers and trees?

Even its keenest advocates say recycling by itself cannot end pollution and waste. The problem lies deeper, they say, in the attitudes of our throwaway society. How much packaging do we need? Disposable products save time, but what do they waste? Can we afford fashions which encourage us to buy new things before the old ones wear out? How much fun, time, and convenience is it worth giving up to save our natural resources?

> 'The bottle is so inexpensive that it is cheaper to throw it away than to go through the reclamation process.' *Vic Hender, United Glass*

A bottle bank – critics of the system say the sound of breaking glass gives it away.

Lead – out of

Lead can damage the brain and even kill – there is no argument about that. The debate is about how much lead is dangerous and where it comes from. Anti-lead campaigners maintain that even the smallest amount can blunt the developing brains of small children and unborn babies. They have singled out lead in petrol as their main object of attack.

3,000 swans die of lead poisoning in Britain every year when they swallow lead fishing weights, says a 1984 report.

Opposite Are city children at risk? In 1979, a study of 2,000 children in the USA found that those with the highest lead levels in their teeth had the greatest problems at school.

Yet petrol is not the most dangerous source of lead pollution. A child who chews old lead paint can become seriously ill; lead solder in tins can leak into food and is banned from baby-food cans; lead pipes can poison drinking water. So why the fuss about petrol? The difference, according to the Royal Commission for Environmental Pollution, is that it is 'a source which the individual can do little to avoid'. 90% of the lead in the air comes from car exhausts and this makes it 'the largest single controllable source of lead for the population as a whole'.

Who's exaggerating? Lead is added to petrol to help car engines run smoothly and efficiently. Lead-free petrol will either mean redesigning car engines or adding something else to petrol instead. This means major changes for the car industry, the petrol industry or maybe both. Lead's defenders – petrol and car makers and the companies, like Britain's Associated Octel, which make lead additives for petrol – claimed that unleaded petrol would be expensive for motorists. Why pay when the danger was still unproved? 'Many committees and commissions have reached the same conclusion,' wrote Associated Octel's house magazine in 1981. 'There is no hazard to health.'

Lead's opponents say this is untrue. They point to growing evidence that children's brains are at risk and that the cost to the motorist will be trivial. You can't get absolute proof without using children as human guinea pigs – but how sure do you have to be? 'Lead may cause population-wide damage,' Australian scientists wrote to *The Melbourne Age* in 1981. 'Shouldn't we remove it first rather than leaving it at large until categorically proved guilty?' Environmentalists say 95% of Britain's inner city children, for example, may be affected by lead in the air, in dust or in vegetables. The lead lobby accuses them of exaggeration.

Ban or cut? Russia banned lead in petrol in 1959 and Japan, America – with some political hiccups – and Australia are phasing it out. 97% of Japanese petrol is now lead-free. Many European countries have already cut lead to the lowest amount on which present cars can run. The EEC is working towards banning lead altogether. Meanwhile governments are taking steps to make unleaded petrol available and to subsidize its cost.

As anti-lead campaigners in some countries turn their attention to paint and water pipes, the petrol debate continues in many others. In the Third World it hasn't even begun – yet their children may be particularly at risk. What are lead fumes from worn-out exhausts doing to children whose minds are already damaged by malnutrition?

their minds **?**

'What civilized government would want to take the risk of endangering its children's minds?'

New York Times, 1982

One Westerner in five dies of cancer. Experts are agreed that environmental factors – the way we live or the world we live in – cause most of these cancers. They disagree, however, about whether pollution or personal lifestyle are more to blame.

Some carcinogens (cancer agents) are well established. Smoking is the largest single cause of cancer in rich countries and is climbing in developing ones. Asbestos dust, vinyl chloride used in the manufacture of plastics, coal tar and radiation are all known killers. But only a fraction of the 80,000 chemicals in commercial use have been tested to see whether they cause cancer. 'It's what we don't know that can really hurt us,' commented a former chief of the US Environmental Protection Agency.

All our own fault? American studies in the '70s gave pollution a large share of the blame for cancer – 30% according to Professor Samuel Epstein. A government study predicted that people who had worked with just six chemicals would soon account for up to a third of the country's cancer cases. Recently, however, supporters of the lifestyle explanation have been gaining ground. British scientists Sir Richard Doll and Richard Peto claim that pollution causes less than 8% of America's cancer deaths, while the real culprits, smoking and fatty foods, cause two-thirds.

Environmentalists and trade unionists fear that governments and industry have seized on these figures as an excuse for less controls. Blaming lifestyle, they say, is like telling people it's their own fault they get cancer. The disease often comes from a number of factors working together – if you smoke and work with asbestos you are at greater risk than if you only do one. Figures often hide this fact.

The most common cancers for men and women in different parts of the world. The fact that cancers differ geographically suggests that they are caused by environmental factors. The World Health Organization estimates there are 5,900,000 cancer cases in the world every year. Two million of these, says WHO, are preventable, and another two million could be cured.

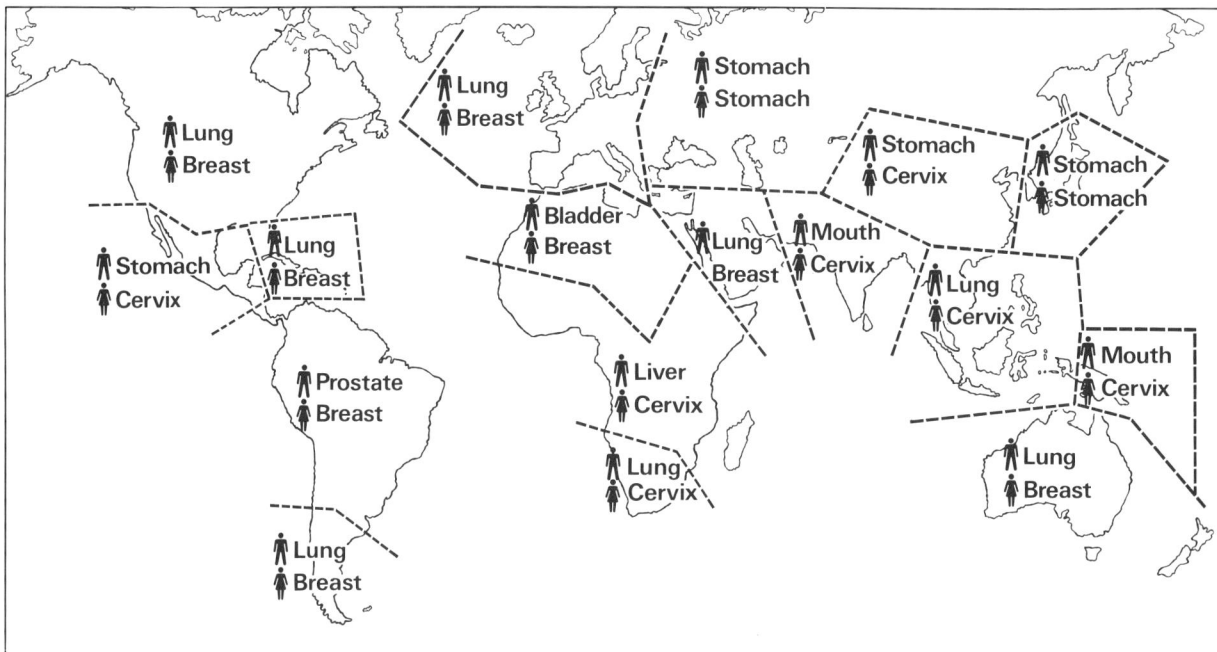

avoid cancer **?**

Most scientists agree that we dare not ignore either pollution or lifestyle. We are at risk from dangerous chemicals at work, in the air, and in our food and water. As cancers can take years to develop and as chemical production has multiplied 300 times since 1935, the main toll of pollution is probably still to come. Each Briton eats over 3 kilos of chemical flavourings, preservatives and colourings a year – some of which may not be safe. In late 1983 baking mixes were rushed off American supermarket shelves when traces of a cancer-linked pesticide were found in grain products: Britons inhale the same chemical from car exhausts.

Foods which fight cancer Smoking, heavy drinking and fatty foods all send people's cancer chances soaring. So may a diet which is low in fibre. An American researcher, Bruce Ames, has found that some foods may contain natural carcinogens – including health food favourites such as alfalfa sprouts, mushrooms and herb teas. Plants produce chemicals to fight off disease and pests, and we probably eat far more of these natural pesticides than we do of manmade ones. 'No human diet can be entirely free of carcinogens,' he writes – but some foods fight against cancer. These include greens, carrots and fruit.

'The "politics of cancer" is dominated on both sides by exaggeration,' says Peto. Experts agree that most cancer is preventable. Is it up to industry or up to us to avoid it?

> '*Cancer is the murderous tribute we have to pay for industrialization.*'
> *Petra Kelly, Green Party, West Germany*

The known killer – cigarette smoking causes some one-fifth of the rich world's cancers.

Is work

T he politics of disease are at their sharpest when it comes to pollution at work. Industries depend on profits and sales – while trade unions, and individual workers, are torn between their jobs and their health. The most notorious health and safety confrontation of the '70s took place in Oklahoma, between Karen Silkwood and the American company Kerr McGee. Her attempts to expose unsafe handling of plutonium in the recycling plant where she worked ended with her death in a car accident.

One tenth of the American men who die of cancer may have their jobs to thank for it, says Professor Samuel Epstein. Nearly 10% of the USA's coal miners had black lung disease (pneumoconiosis) in the '70s, while a quarter of Bolivia's tin miners had silicosis, another lung disease caused by dust. One of the rich world's most common industrial diseases is deafness.

Fatal time-lags Unlike industrial accidents, which according to one estimate killed or injured at least 1 in 40 US workers in 1971, work-related illnesses may only catch up with people after they retire. Their causes can be hard to prove and both industry and workers have an interest in not jumping to conclusions. 'Corporations, executives and owners, and often the workers themselves, weigh immediate gain against the uncertain prospect that diseases might develop decades later,' writes Erik Eckholm.

The costs of delay can be heavy. Coal tar fumes were first linked with cancer 200 years ago – yet in the 1970s coke-oven workers in many countries were still inhaling them and dying of cancer at ten times the rate of other steel workers.

The dangers of working with asbestos have been known since the 1890s, when 50 employees of a French asbestos-weaving factory died within five years of its opening. In subsequent years it was proved that asbestos dust could cause the fatal disease asbestosis and also cancers. But it was not until the 1970s that most countries began to take the threat seriously. Meanwhile tens of thousands of workers and their families had died.

The asbestos debate The British example is typical. By 1977 the country's asbestos industry was worth £200 million and employed 20,000 people. Another 100,000 handled asbestos regularly at work. In one Yorkshire factory, which in 30 years' operation was never prosecuted, 260 workers or members of their families had become ill and 70 had died. Government standards for asbestos dust in the workplace were being attacked on the grounds that no level of exposure was safe. *The Times* pinpointed the central issue: 'To what extent, if any, should jobs and national prosperity be put before the lives of those who die prematurely because of asbestos-related disease?'

By 1983 public opinion had forced the industry to look at new alternatives. 'We can't survive unless we change,' commented one asbestos manufacturer. Most countries are left with the problem of what to do about all the asbestos fireproofing and insulation installed in buildings in less careful days. Is it safer to leave it where it is, or risk putting even more dust into the air by removing it?

Whether the threat is noise, chemicals or dust, the issues are much the same. Is there

Opposite Mining is one of the world's most dangerous jobs. 'There is overwhelming evidence that coal mining still uses up men and discards them to an exceptional extent,' said the British medical journal, *The Lancet,* in 1974.

> *'It's like a major war. The casualties, however, aren't fighting, but just trying to make a living.'* George Wald, US biochemist

a health hazard **?**

any justification for risking workers' lives?
Are high wages – when paid – an adequate
compensation? Should some materials be
banned outright or are safety limits possible?
Should rules be so tight that workers can't cut
corners? How much do workers have a right
to know the dangers they may face?

*'An immediate ban on all asbestos products
would be certain to cause a substantial
number of deaths.'* Asbestos Information Committee, 1976

'Whatever causes stomach cancer it is most unlikely to be nitrates.'

Dr D. D. Bryson, Imperial Chemical Industries, 1983

A nitrate timebomb?

Are farmers poisoning our children's water supplies? This is one of today's most emotive pollution issues, for it links two of our biggest horrors – hunger and cancer.

Since the '40s, world food production has soared, mainly thanks to chemical fertilizers. Between 1948 and 1981 world grain production doubled and world fertilizer use multiplied eight times. Fertilizers help plants by giving them extra supplies of the minerals they need to grow. But the plants can't use all they're given, and the leftover nitrates wash away with the rain into rivers and trickle down through the earth into the groundwater reserves which supply much of our drinking water.

Agricultural run-off finds its way quickly into surface waters, boosting their nitrate levels at some times of the year. This can cause overenrichment (see page 21) and affect drinking water supplies. The nitrates take much longer to reach the groundwater – travelling a metre or two a year through some rocks and soils. If the water table is deep, it may take up to 50 years for the nitrates to arrive. So, environmentalists say, we are still waiting for the nitrate timebomb which was set when fertilizer use leapt after the Second World War. Meanwhile high nitrate levels have already been found in shallower groundwaters beneath French and German farming areas.

Is there a health risk? Whether any of this really matters is a subject of heated debate. High nitrate levels in water can kill babies – though this is rare. Many scientists are more worried about a possible cancer risk to the public at large, for chemical reactions in the body may turn nitrates into substances which cause cancer in animals. Nitrates also reach us in vegetables and in preserved foods such as ham, bacon and some cheeses.

Those who believe there is a danger point out that nations who eat a lot of nitrates have high stomach cancer rates – Japan is world leader in both. The people of Aalborg, Denmark, are like their neighbours in Aarhus in almost every way – except that they have more nitrates in their drinking water and more often get stomach cancer.

Others stress that there is no firm proof that nitrates and cancer are linked. East Anglia, with one of Britain's highest nitrate levels, has some of her lowest stomach cancer rates. And why, they ask, is stomach cancer decreasing worldwide just as fertilizer use is rising? A sceptical report in 1979 described the evidence as 'weak and contradictory'; but concluded that it would be 'prudent' to reduce our nitrate intake 'as far as reasonably possible'.

What can be done? Nitrate levels can be cut by treating water or by getting farmers to stop overusing fertilizers. Both may be necessary, for nitrates which took decades to reach the groundwater will take decades to flush out. However any long-term answer, say environmentalists, depends on farmers. New farming methods which use fertilizers more efficiently might not only save the environment – but save the farmers money as well.

Without chemical fertilizers, the world's food output would fall by at least a third. But after a certain point, extra fertilizer cannot improve a crop's yield. According to Worldwatch's Lester Brown, the fields of Holland (*opposite*) are reaching saturation point. The same is happening in Japan and the North American cornbelt.

Are pesticides

The anti-malaria campaign of the 1950s and '60s saved 15 million lives – thanks largely to pesticides. Without pesticides the US would lose nearly a tenth of her crops. 30% of the world's agricultural potential is lost because of insects, weeds, fungus and animals.

All this, say manufacturers, is an argument for more and better chemicals. Environmentalists say we are already using too many.

Out of control? At least 14,000 US farmers are poisoned by pesticides every year, campaigners say, and some show unusually high cancer rates. The public are at risk from accidents and from pesticide residues in their food. Aerial spray can drift and damage nearby fields. Some crops are sprayed unnecessarily, 'just to be safe' or to make produce look better in the shops. An American study claims that farmers could cut pesticide use by up to a half, without losing anything.

Overuse can give pests a chance to become immune. In 1954, 25 of the world's pest species could resist pesticides; now over 400 can. Mosquitos' resistance is one reason why malaria is on the increase again in the Third World.

These arguments have made environmentalists press for tighter controls on the pesticide industry. On the other hand, manufacturers say their products are safe if used correctly, and too expensive for anyone to overuse.

> '*We see nothing wrong in helping the hungry world to eat.*' *Executive of Velsicol, USA*

Do farmers know what they are doing when they spray their crops? A recent study in one area found that on most farms there was no-one trained to use pesticides, and few took proper safety precautions. Over a quarter said they found pesticide information hard to follow. If this is the case in a developed country, ask campaigners, what happens in countries where farmworkers are not educated?

a pest ?

The effects of persistent pesticides like DDT caused an outcry in the 1960s. Birds of prey, like this sparrowhawk, built up high levels of poison in their bodies when they fed on birds and animals which had eaten poisoned grain. Many died and others laid such fragile eggs that the species began to decline. Most uses of these pesticides are now banned in the developed world – but the less persistent pesticides which have replaced them are more dangerous to people.

The Third World Developing nations also use large quantities of pesticides – and risks there are increased by illiteracy, poor working conditions and poverty. Researchers tell horror stories of lethal chemicals being served out by hand; pesticide drums being used for water; fields being sprayed while people are working in them. One person in the Third World is poisoned by a pesticide every minute.

When a dangerous chemical is banned in the rich world, there is little to stop its makers from exporting it. According to US law, importers must be told about any dangerous chemical being shipped to them. Environmentalists want this system tightened and applied worldwide. US businessmen say it makes America 'the world's nursemaid' and companies argue that hunger, not the environment, is the Third World's problem.

Some Third World spokesmen agree; others say they cannot afford to test chemicals themselves and must draw on the rich world's experience. 'If these products aren't good enough for the United States, they can't be good enough for us,' said Mexico's Under-Secretary of the Environment in 1981. The United Nations Environment Programme has set up an international register of toxic chemicals to provide information for importers.

A middle road? There are three main standpoints in the debate – the 'no chemicals' approach of organic farmers and gardeners; the pro-pesticides view; and a middle road which argues for careful use of pesticides alongside other ways of controlling pests. These include encouraging the pest's natural enemies, breeding resistant types of crop, and using traditional methods of farming. 'Any attempt to discuss pesticide use in the Third World in terms of pesticides versus no pesticides is merely to obscure the real issue,' writes Oxfam's David Bull.

> *'These very toxic pesticides are being thrown all over the world and there's no control over it.'*
> *Harold Hubbard, UN Pan-American Health Organization*

Can the poor

In the Third World pollution is a mass murderer. Saving the thousands who die each day because of dirty water is a major development priority.

Other pollution concerns sometimes seem to conflict with development. How much should the Third World worry about the possible dangers from pesticides and fertilizers, when they need food so badly? How important are clean air or safe working conditions when hundreds of millions are unemployed? Can developing countries afford to bother about the long-term hazards of fossil fuels? Is pollution just the rich world's problem?

Pollution can overwhelm people who live on the margins of survival – like the inhabitants of the shanties clustered around the Union Carbide factory in Bhopal, India, where the world's worst chemical disaster took place in 1984. The cloud of methylisocyanate released killed and injured thousands. When factory wastes destroyed Malaysian fisheries in the '70s, incomes in the fishing village of Kuala Juru fell by four-fifths. When pesticides drive fish out of the rice fields, Asian farmers lose their main source of protein. In overcrowded, polluted cities, the poor are the first to suffer. Just breathing in Mexico City is as dangerous as smoking 40 cigarettes a day, says a city health officer. Some 7 million of its people have chronic bronchitis.

Importing pollution Banned pesticides are not the only pollutants which find markets in the Third World. The debate on dangerous chemicals and technologies is similar to the pesticides debate. Some Third World spokesmen – like Kenya's deputy environment minister – say their countries are 'being taken for a ride' by the rich world. Others say what they import is their own affair and accuse those who want tighter controls of 'environmental imperialism'. How real is the danger that companies will use developing countries as hazardous waste tips or pollution havens?

Since it is cheaper to build non-polluting factories than adapt old ones, some experts say the Third World can avoid the mistakes of the developed world. Rich countries have discovered how expensive cleaning up pollution can be. 'For the Third World to try to cut corners in development by wishing away the pollution challenge would be bad economics as well as bad ecology,' comments Erik Eckholm.

Paying for the rich? In some cases developing countries are being asked to pay for the rich world's overconsumption. The UN's Mediterranean Action Plan ran temporarily aground when countries were asked to control the amount of pollution they put into the sea. 'It seemed very much to the poorer countries like a plot by the rich countries,' a UN official told *Newsweek*. Why should the poorer countries cramp their industries to save a sea they didn't pollute in the first place? The same arguments could apply to rising carbon dioxide levels in the atmosphere. If fossil fuels threaten the world's climate, should the rich world cut back all the more, so as to let the Third World use the fuels they need?

In the long run all mankind is in the same boat. The Third World may feel more committed to keeping it afloat, says Colombia's Margerita de Botero, when 'we stop being second-class passengers'.

Opposite Pollution to these Colombians is the smoke from burning rubbish. For many of their compatriots it is filthy water – the main reason the country's infant mortality is nearly one in ten. In cities like Cubatao, Brazil – the continent's largest industrial complex – the worst pollution comes from factories. Cubatao's factories belch out nearly 1,000 tonnes of pollutants a day, and a quarter of the city's poorest people have breathing diseases as a result.

'We in the developing world do not consider acid rains and other pollutants a major problem.'
S. Ambalavaner, Sri Lanka National Council

afford to care **?**

'For the rich, pollution is the result of progress; for the poor, of poverty.'

Sunil Kumar Roy, Indian environmentalist

Can the rich

President Reagan came to office in 1981 promising US industry to 'get Washington off your backs'. His administration was soon locked in combat with environmentalists over lead restrictions and clean air laws, which it claimed were stunting industrial growth.

Each new pollution discovery brings fears of high prices, job losses and factory closures. In the early '70s German petrol companies said lead limits would put 25p a gallon on petrol prices. In 1984 Britain's Coal Board chairman said tighter acid rain controls could cripple industry, and officials of the Confederation of British Industry (CBI) warned that plans to clean up the Mersey could frighten new firms away from a depressed area.

> **'The cost of action is high, but the cost of inaction is higher.'**
> Charles Caccia, Canadian Environment Minister, 1983

The cost of pollution Environmentalists maintain that these claims are exaggerated. The German leads laws, for example, in the end added nothing to the cost of petrol. Pollution, they say, is expensive in itself. The pesticide company which poisoned America's James River in the early '70s could have saved itself over $13 million in damages if it had spent $200,000 on pollution control. It cost millions of dollars to clean up after 'midnight dumpers' sprayed chemicals along North Carolina roads in 1978. They could have been safely disposed of for $100,000. Clean-up nearly always costs more than prevention, and fitting new anti-pollution equipment is usually more expensive than starting out with it.

The human costs of pollution are harder to put a price on. How much is a child's mind worth – or a worker's health? What is the cash value of a river that doesn't smell? Money saved is harder to count than money spent, but the US Council on Environmental Quality (CEQ) reckoned that for $17 billion spent on air pollution control in 1978, the country saved itself $21.4 billion in medical bills, repairs and damaged crops.

Big business Many firms have found that pollution prevention pays. The huge American company 3M saved $97 million in six

afford to care ?

years through recycling and conservation, and a French oil refinery made an extra £430,000 a year when it started to sell its wastes. France, for example, could save $1 billion a year in imports if it used its wastes and by-products better, says Michael Royston of Geneva's Environmental Management Centre.

Small ailing companies are more at risk – but few firms have ever closed because of pollution regulations alone. In 1977 the CEQ estimated that for 20,000 jobs lost in the USA because of pollution laws, some 2 million had been created in pollution control.

Pollution control was Brazil's fastest growing industry in the late '70s. In the early '70s the Swedish government pulled their country out of a recession by offering large subsidies for plants to install anti-pollution technology. With a world market in control technology and environmental services valued at $100 billion, there is a strong incentive for countries to get ahead in their own fight against pollution, so as to have the technology to sell to those who lag behind.

In the long run, environmentalists believe the rich world cannot afford to ignore pollution. In the short run, pollution prevention can be costly. Who should have to pay for it?

'[The Environmental Protection Agency] has rules that would practically shut down the economy if they were put into effect.'

David Stockman, US politician

Pollution is blamed for the bare hillside behind this smelter in Australia (*far left*) and for the death of this tree in Germany's Black Forest (*left*). Is the landscape worth the costs of pollution control?

E veryone benefits from a clean environment – but somebody has to pay for it. Lead-free city air could give millions of children fuller lives – but cost petrol additive workers their jobs. Is it fair for particular industries, workers and consumers to have to pay for the health and environment of society as a whole?

In theory most industrialized countries believe that polluters should pay their own pollution control or clean-up expenses. Industries then pass on these costs to their customers. In America in the early '70s, pollution controls increased food prices by 1% and petrol prices by 4.6%.

A licence to pollute? Some 15% of the Japanese steel industry's investment in plant and equipment between 1970 and 1978 went on pollution control. Meeting pollution standards is costly; so if the fines for breaking pollution laws are not high enough, some firms may decide it is cheaper to go on polluting. In 1983, when a British paper mill

'The citizen pays either as consumer or as taxpayer or as victim.' Barbara Ward and René Dubos, Only One Earth

A polluter who cannot pay? In March 1984, this smokeless fuel plant in Abercwmboi in South Wales told an industrial tribunal that it was running at a loss and could not afford new anti-pollution equipment. Locals complain that they get the smoke while other people get the clean fuel. The tribunal upheld the firm's case.

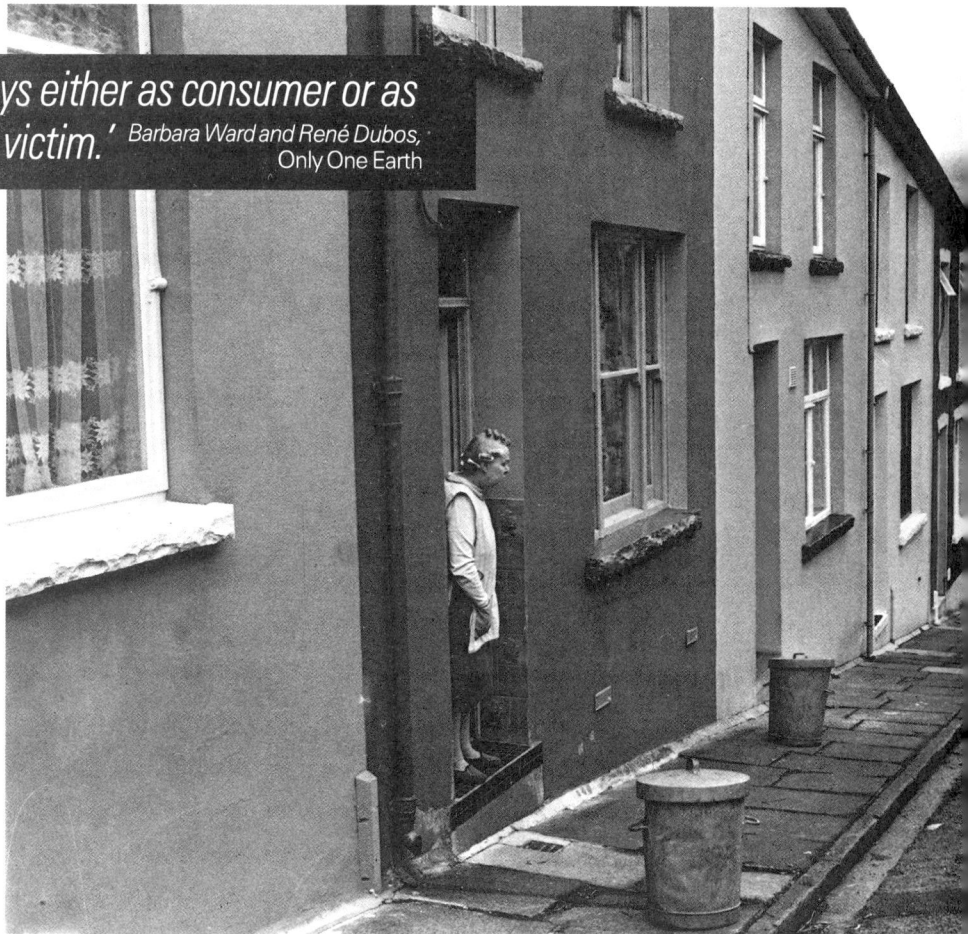

pay ?

was fined only £750 for poisoning the River Don, it saw no reason to stop.

Some economists think pollution taxes would work better than laws. These too may become a 'licence to pollute'; but some systems seem to work well. Factories along Germany's Ruhr river are charged for the amount of pollution they put into the river and the money pays for water treatment. A similar system in France allows the money collected to be paid back to companies to subsidize pollution control investments.

Japan extends the polluter pays principle to health. In 1979, 73,189 Japanese were receiving compensation for diseases caused by air pollution or by mercury, cadmium or arsenic pollution. The money came from polluting industries and – for diseases linked to air pollution – from car taxes.

Can't pay, won't pay? Problems begin when industries can't afford to pay. In 1983 a parliamentary report advised the British government to help struggling industries to buy new pollution control equipment. Without subsidies, commented one submission, 'unacceptable choices between employment and environmental quality will be presented to local communities'. In the early '70s the Swedish government paid 50-70% of the cost of equipping old industries to cut pollution. Several countries give tax concessions to firms installing pollution controls, and some offer loans or grants.

What happens when polluters are hard to trace? Who should pay to clean up the forgotten waste tips scattered around many countries? After the evacuation of Lekkerkerk in 1980, the Dutch government promised to deal with 300 similar chemical dumps. Environmentalists were outraged by the suggestion that taxpayers rather than industry should pay two-thirds of the bill. The US set up a hazardous dump clean-up fund in 1980, financed mostly by a tax on chemical raw materials and partly by government.

Goods cost money to make – and they also have environmental costs. Should car buyers, for instance, just pay what it costs to make their cars, or what it costs to make them without harming the environment? The former, say environmentalists, just means we are subsidizing pollution. How can we know whether something is good value until we know the full cost of its manufacture and use? In the end, 'polluters pay' means 'consumers pay'. Do we want to?

> 'Industry created the mess. They should pay the bill.'
>
> *Jan Henselmans,*
> *Dutch environmentalist*

49

Controlling

Imagine a factory in the middle of the Sahara desert, hundreds of miles from anywhere. Would it matter what pollution it released into the atmosphere? Should pollution standards be the same everywhere or do local circumstances make a difference? This question has divided the European Community, and taxed the minds of planners everywhere.

Does geography change things? The row in the EEC arose over the Community's attempts to control the pollution of rivers and seas by dangerous wastes. Its draft directive suggested uniform rules for the most toxic wastes, regardless of the environment into which they were being released. Britain claimed this was illogical. Surely it made a difference whether you were putting pollution into a clean, fast-flowing British river or into a heavily polluted river like the Rhine, which wound slowly through France, Germany and Holland and provided 20 million people with drinking water? Why should Britain, surrounded by turbulent tidal seas, which quickly bear away her wastes, be limited by what Italy could put into the sluggish, filthy Mediterranean?

Other European countries retorted that such arguments would put British firms at an unfair advantage. Why should they be allowed to spend less on pollution control just because of an accident of geography? In the end a compromise was reached – countries could choose whether they adapted their standards to each situation or imposed the same controls on all companies. Britain alone opted for the first choice.

The best practicable means? Britain is the odd-country-out in world pollution control, putting more trust in co-operation between control bodies and industry than in the bans and rigid standards preferred by the US, Japan and most of Europe. Bans can be hard to enforce, and legal standards have to go back to parliament to be changed if new risks or controls are discovered.

Britain lays great emphasis on 'the best practicable means' – pollution control methods agreed between factory inspectors and industry, taking local conditions, finance and available technology into account. At best this system is an elastic band, which tightens as the need arises. At its worst, it is a gigantic loophole for firms who say they cannot afford to stop polluting.

At the other extreme from the 'best practicable means' is the 'best available technology' policy, often enforced by the US and Japan. This insists that polluters use the latest technology to cut pollution as much as possible, regardless of cost or the needs of the environment. Critics say this is impracticable and imposes unnecessary burdens on industry.

Both sides agree that it is much better to install pollution controls in factories when they are built, rather than to add them later. Adding new equipment to old factories is extremely expensive, and cleaning up pollution can create pollution of its own. Obviously, the best solution is to design factories which can reuse their wastes and create little pollution at all.

When standards for existing factories are tightened up, many environmentalists would agree with industry that a flexible approach works best, as it makes constant improvements possible. The one essential – which they say is often missing – is the will to make it work. Without it, as one commentator warns the 'best practicable means' can easily degenerate into the 'cheapest tolerable means'.

> '*A co-operative, pragmatic, cross-sectoral and preventative approach will see us through.*' Giles Shaw, former British environment minister

pollution?

Methods of pollution regulation

Environmental quality objectives and standards ask polluters to trim their effluents to the state of the environment receiving them. Objectives usually give general aims – for instance, that a river should be suitable for migrating fish; standards state the maximum level of pollutant allowed in the river.

Emission and effluent standards control what goes out through the factory chimney or waste pipe. They may vary from factory to factory or be universal.

Product standards regulate the amount of certain substances allowed in the finished product – for instance, the amount of lead in petrol.

Total emission standards state the total amount of pollution allowed in one country or area, such as this port in Japan. Firms can then share out the quota between them.

'I just hope that my grandchildren don't look back on this generation and say, "No wonder they had problems – look at all the chemicals carelessly introduced into the environment, uncontrolled." '

Douglas Costle, US EPA, 1978

51

'If rational considerations alone were involved one would conclude that this pursuit of safety had gone too far.'
N. L. Franklin, Nuclear Power Co., 1976

Worth the risk?

If you lived on Canvey Island, England, in 1981, you were nearly 10 times more likely to be killed by an industrial accident than in a car crash. A serious accident at a liquefied natural gas plant could wipe out half a city, say environmentalists – and the US, Japan, France, Spain, Germany, Holland and Britain all have plants or terminals in larger cities. Bhophal and Chernobyl have shaken public confidence in the safety of chemical and nuclear plants. Pollution probably ups our chances of getting cancer. Should we accept these risks as an inevitable price of industrial development?

Once in 10 million years? It has often been said that people's ideas of risk are exaggerated. We all take big chances every day without even thinking about them. The world loses 250,000 lives on the road every year – but this doesn't keep many of us at home. A serious nuclear reactor accident is only likely once in every 10 million reactor years, says the nuclear industry. Yet people who cheerfully take their lives in their hands by hang-gliding, heavy smoking or cycling through the rush hour wouldn't dream of living near one. Isn't this illogical? 'The current exaggerated, if not maniacal, attitude of some people towards our environment is very damaging to our well-being,' said Lord Rothschild in a controversial lecture on risk in 1978.

Environmentalists dispute the 'one chance in 10 million' approach to risks on various grounds. Firstly, they say, such figures are unreliable – miss out one possibility and the whole ratio is upset. Secondly, likelihood is only one side of risk – what about the scale of the possible disaster? A major nuclear accident could not only kill outright, but cause thousands of cancer deaths years later and genetic defects for generations. And surely, they say, there is something different about dangers you

choose for yourself – like hang-gliding – and ones you cannot avoid – like poisons in your drinking water? Even if comparisons between risks are fair, are they relevant? You may be more likely to die of 'flu than of radiation – but does one danger make the other acceptable?

Weighing the advantages Governments have to balance risks against needs. If we are going to run out of energy, nuclear power may be a solution. Pesticides may kill – but starvation is even more lethal.

Such calculations are upset if there are realistic alternatives to the dangers. Sometimes no-one starts looking for these until a risk has been vetoed. When Japan decided to control pollution from cars, says Dr Tokue Shibata of Tokyo's Metropolitan Research Institute, the industry said the new exhaust targets were impossible. 'We said, "So long as you do not stop this kind of pollution you must stop automobile production." Suddenly an excellent new invention comes up!'

Is it fair to put those who work in a hazardous industry or live near one at risk because the industry benefits society? And what happens when there is a choice between them? An accident at one European methane gas terminal could kill 250,000 people, it was estimated in 1981. An inspector suggested that if the plant could not be shut, it should be fitted with ignition devices on its boundaries so that any escaping gas would explode before it reached the general public. 'It is surely better to risk the lives of a comparatively small workforce, who benefit from being there, rather than others who benefit less,' he maintained.

A British study on risk assessment in 1977 made one major recommendation – that those in danger should have a 'powerful voice' in deciding whether a risk should be allowed.

> 'Every chemical company has problems and I personally wouldn't live next to one.'
> Director, Abba Chemicals

Opposite 200 people were killed in Spain in 1978 when fire swept through this campsite after a tanker carrying liquefied gas spilled its load. Liquefying gas concentrates it considerably, making it easier to store and transport. It could be the answer to gas shortages. But is it worth the risk?

Before people at risk can have a 'powerful voice' in decision-making, they need to know the facts, which are often uncertain. Is it fair to tell people about dangers which are not yet proved – or is it unfair not to?

Tests, scares and delays The most definite test of a pollutant is to see what it does to people. Deaths among workers in dangerous industries, for instance, have often acted as early warning systems for the public. But no-one would seriously maintain that this 'body-counting' is acceptable. Instead scientists screen chemicals before they reach people, using expensive – and not always decisive – tests on animals.

Scientists can now use bacteria to select chemicals which may cause cancer and need further testing. Proving a one in a thousand risk needs thousands of animals, several years and can cost well over £100,000. A recent study by the National Research Council found that only 10% of the pesticides in use in America had been thoroughly tested.

Waiting for proof can lead to fatal delays. Doing without it may lead to scares. Environmentalists say that many dangers cannot be proved for sure. If we wait, it may be too late. The more cautious stress the risks of banning products or processes unnecessarily.

Scares have ranged from the ridiculous – does coloured loo paper poison rivers? – to the tragic – nine American women had abortions because of an alleged link between

> *'I believe in informing the public, but not in giving them figures they can't interpret. People can become scared of figures.'*
> *Frank Ireland, former Chief Alkali Inspector, 1977*

to know ?

spray adhesives and birth defects which was later disproved. Sometimes mistakes are made. In 1970 several countries banned cyclamate sweeteners because tests showed they caused cancer in rats. Dieters switched to saccharin. Seven years later it turned out that the test rats had been fed saccharin as well as cyclamates. Which caused the cancer? Could the wrong sweetener have been banned?

Secrecy – for whose sake? Scares are one of the main reasons given for not publishing pollution details. Advocates of secrecy are particularly strong in Britain. They say disclosure of the facts could lead to panic and pressure for unnecessary controls.

Some companies fear that if their competitors knew what went into their products – or even what they threw away – they could copy them. Information about hazardous factories, says Britain's Chemical Industries Association, 'would prove invaluable in the hands of terrorists'.

Environmentalists argue that people find secrets more frightening than the truth, that trade secrets can easily be cracked anyway, and that polluters have an interest in keeping quiet about what they are doing. They say that people have a 'right to know'.

> **'Secrecy fuels fear.'** *Royal Commission on Environmental Pollution, 1984*

A ghost town? Police guard the entrance to Seveso, northern Italy, in July 1976 after an accident in a chemical reactor engulfed the town in a cloud of vapour. It was five days before anyone realized that the cloud contained the lethal poison dioxin – and two weeks before people were evacuated from some of the contaminated areas.

Politics

Can we save the environment by going on as we are, only more cleanly? Or do we need to rethink the whole way our world is run, as some radical environmentalists believe?

Most pollution issues cause clashes between economic interests on one side and health and conservation concerns on the other. Pollution, because it involves money and power, is a political issue. Pressure groups like the Campaign for Lead-Free Air and Friends of the Earth use every means within the law to change government and industrial policies. Some groups, like Greenpeace, take direct action which brings them into conflict with the law. Environmental groups in America have put their weight behind political candidates – and successfully campaigned against Reagan's anti-environmentalist Interior Secretary James Watt, who resigned in 1983.

As many of the debates in this book show, most environmentalists believe that the problems of pollution and waste can still be solved within the present political framework.

A threat to society? Some commentators, like the right-wing US Republican Study Committee, have accused environmentalists of deliberately undermining energy development and economic prosperity. 'Environmentalists are members of an élite and affluent class, largely insulated from the consequences of resource development and economic growth,' they claimed in 1982.

Many environmentalists would deny the claim that they were out to upturn society. Radicals, however, believe this is just what is needed. 'It is all too easy to demonstrate concern for the environment without in any way upsetting the *status quo*,' writes British environmentalist Jonathon Porritt.

In several countries this radical wing has founded Green parties to fight in local and national elections. The Germans, Europe's most successful Greens, won 28 seats in a general election in 1983; while Brice Lalonde, leader of France's Friends of the Earth, won 1 million votes in the French presidential elections in 1981.

A Green world Green parties believe both socialism and capitalism have got it wrong because they concentrate on economic growth. Materialism is destroying our planet, they say, and is the root of unemployment and of the world gulf between rich and poor. Society needs reorganizing on a basis where

'The spectre of environment-alism haunts America.'
Republican report, 1982

and pollution ?

everybody gets enough – and is satisfied with that. The Green package includes unilateral disarmament and a total rejection of nuclear power; and an emphasis on decentralization and small, co-operative, businesses. 'We have stepped into the system in order to change it,' says Petra Kelly of the German Greens.

Green politics question the assumptions of middle of the road environmentalists as well as of polluters. Exploiting nature is linked to exploiting people, say Greens, so it is no good worrying about wildlife and ignoring social justice. 'To solve the environmental crisis we must solve the problem of poverty, racial injustice and war,' writes pioneer American ecologist Barry Commoner. 'The debt to nature cannot be paid, person by person, in recycled bottles or ecologically sound habits, but in the ancient coin of social justice.'

> 'The only alternative to the politics of exploitation is the politics of ecology.'
> Jonathon Porritt, British environmentalist

German demonstrators march against acid rain, carrying a coffin and a small tree damaged by pollution. 'First the woods die, then mankind,' states the slogan on the cross.

Everybody's

'If present trends continue, the world in 2000 will be more crowded, more polluted, less stable ecologically and more vulnerable to disruption than the world we live in now,' warned the American *Global 2000* report in 1980. Pollution is not the only environmental threat to our planet – but it may be the one we in the West can do most about.

We cannot live without creating pollution – even if it is only the smoke from the wood-stove on a self-sufficient farm. But we can do a great deal to reduce it. It will demand changes – for even at a slow rate of growth, according to another report in 1980, present pollution controls in the industrialized world are not strong enough to stop pollution increasing.

So what can we do? First we can ask the questions. What chemicals are we using – and are they worth it? Are conditions at home or work really safe, or is someone taking shortcuts? What pollutants are particularly dangerous to small children? What is the local factory putting into the river and the air? What is finding its way onto the local rubbish dump? If something is wrong you can join up with others to put pressure on industry or government.

Asking the questions Pollution reminds us that humanity is interdependent. The crisp packet I drop becomes someone else's problem; so does the sewage a city flushes untreated into a river; the mercury a factory

Isolated – but part of an interdependent world?

problem **?**

dumps in the sea; the acids a power station puffs into the air. The fate of the climate or oceans will determine the future of all humanity.

Consumer power Governments all over the world tend to think in the short term – the immediate crisis, the next election. Pollution acts slowly – lakes take years to die and cancers can take decades to grow. Politicians think we won't vote for them if they offer us a cleaner environment rather than a higher standard of living. 'There are no votes in sewage,' they say. But a national opinion poll in the early '80s revealed that one in five voters would readily consider switching their vote to a main party which committed itself to wasting less natural resources.

> **'Environment is people and people are environment.'**
> Aurelio Peccei, Club of Rome, 1982

Pollution is linked to our lifestyles. If we want goods we can enjoy for a while and then throw away, industry will produce them for us, taking short cuts to keep the prices down. Are we ready to pay for clean air and water? Do we really want a society where things last? Do we judge ourselves and each other by what we have – or by what we are like? Of course we need money to survive and possessions to enjoy – but how much is enough?

'People's perception of environmental problems has improved,' said the United Nations Environment Programme, in its review of the 10 years since the Stockholm conference. 'It is less clear that many groups have adapted their lifestyles in response.' Whose problem is pollution – someone else's, or our own?

> **'At root we are all polluters.'**
> Maurice Ash, Dartington Hall Trust

Reference

Glossary

Acid rain – Rain polluted with sulphuric and nitric acids.

Carbon dioxide (CO_2) – Gas released by plants and animals, when organisms decay and when wood or fossil fuels are burnt. Causes the so-called greenhouse effect.

Carcinogen – Substance which can produce cancer.

Chlorofluorocarbons (CFCs) – Chemicals used in aerosols, refrigeration and some sorts of foam. Thought to threaten the ozone layer and add to the greenhouse effect.

DDT (Dichlorodiphenyltrichloroethane) – A persistent pesticide.

Dioxin – A family of highly poisonous chemicals, some of them produced when certain herbicides are made.

Ecology – The relationship between living things and their environment.

Ecosystem – A community of living things within a certain area, which interact with each other and their environment.

Effluent – Liquid waste.

Emission – Gaseous waste.

Fast breeder – Nuclear reactor which converts those uranium atoms which cannot be used as fuel into plutonium, which can.

Food chain – A series of living things which eat each other. For instance, a fox may eat a bird which has eaten an insect which ate a plant. Pollutants can pass up the food chain from the plant to the fox.

Fossil fuels – Fuels derived from animals and plants which died millions of years ago. They include coal, oil and gas.

Greenhouse effect – The way in which some gases trap the sun's heat within the Earth's atmosphere, thus possibly leading to a warmer climate.

Liquefied natural gas – Natural gas converted into a liquid for transport or storage. This process concentrates it 600 times. Extremely flammable.

Nitrate – Salt essential to plant growth which is formed from nitrogen.

Nitrogen oxides (NOx) – Gases released when fuels – including petrol – are burnt. A cause of acid rain and photochemical smog.

Organochlorines – A group of persistent chemicals which include DDT and some other pesticides, and PCBs.

Overenrichment – The process of decay which begins when algae in rivers and lakes are overfertilized by farm run-off and sewage work effluents. Also known as 'eutrophication'.

Ozone – A form of oxygen with three atoms per molecule instead of two. In city air ozone is a dangerous pollutant, but the atmospheric ozone layer is part of our life support system, screening out the ultraviolet rays of the sun.

PCBs (Polychlorinated biphenyls) and *PBB (Polybrominated biphenyl)* – Persistent chemicals used in plastics, in transformer cooling oils and as fire-retardants. The use of PCBs is now restricted.

Photochemical smog – Dangerous smog created by the interaction of sunlight and exhaust fumes.

Sulphur dioxide (SO_2) – A gas released by burning coal and oil which contain sulphur. A major cause of acid rain and air pollution.

Further reading

Down to Earth by Erik Eckholm (Pluto Press, 1982). A readable and up-to-date discussion of environmental issues in the '70s and '80s. Covers pollution and conservation as part of the struggle to create a more just global society.

Friends of the Earth Guide to Pollution by Brian Price (Maurice Temple Smith, 1983). A concise guide to pollution in Britain.

Only one Earth by Barbara Ward and René Dubos (Penguin Books, 1972). The book that launched the global environmental debate. Some of the facts are now out of date, but it is worth reading as an introduction to the issues and to the spirit of environmentalism.

Rich World, Poor World by Geoffrey Lean (George Allen and Unwin, 1978). Deals with the gulf between rich and poor nations as well as conservation and pollution. Clear chapters on nuclear and alternative energy sources, energy conservation and chemical pollutants.

The Environment – a dictionary of the world about us by Geoffrey Holister and Andrew Porteous (Arrow Books, 1976). Useful reference book for technical terms and issues.

Carbon Dioxide, Climate and Man, by John Gribbin (Earthscan/IIED, 1981). Originally a briefing paper for journalists, it is a manageable summary of the carbon dioxide debate.

Water, Sanitation and Health – for all? (Earthscan/IIED, 1981). Detailed introduction to the possibilities and problems of the UN clean water decade.

Two other Earthscan publications provide studies of the water problem in specific places – *A million villages, a million decades?* (1983) looks at two villages in South India; *Who puts the water in the taps?* (1983) gives examples of community projects.

The *New Scientist* weekly magazine is a good source for current developments in the pollution field.

For clear pamphlets on the technical side of nuclear power and on the industry's point of view, write to the United Kingdom Atomic Energy Authority, 11 Charles II St, London SW1Y 4QP.

For the electricity industry's view on energy options in general, write to the Central Electricity Generating Board, Sudbury House, 15 Newgate St, London EC1A 7AU.

Living with Energy by the Lothian Energy Group (1983) gives an imaginative summary of energy conservation and renewable energy in Britain. It can be ordered, with other information, from the Department of Energy, Distribution Unit, Room 1312, Thames House South, Millbank, London SW1P 4QJ.

Useful addresses

Friends of the Earth has 20,000 supporters in Britain and 250 local groups. It campaigns against pollution and nuclear power and for the environment. Information from Friends of the Earth, 377 City Road, London EC1.

Greenpeace takes 'uncompromising but peaceful action in defence of the environment'. It has campaigned against nuclear weapon testing, the dumping of nuclear and other dangerous wastes at sea, nuclear power, acid rain and the killing of whales and seals. Information from Greenpeace, 30-31 Islington Green, London N1 8XE

CLEAR (The Campaign for Lead-free Air) campaigns against lead pollution. Information from 3 Endsleigh Street, London WC1H 0DD.

The Green Party, Britain's environmental political party (formerly the Ecology Party), can be contacted at 10 Station Parade, Balham High Road, Balham, London SW12 9AZ.

Places to visit

Power stations Many CEGB power stations have open days and most can be visited by groups by appointment. They include coal- and oil-fired power stations, and nuclear and hydroelectric plants. Ring the regional office of the CEGB for details. To visit the wind turbine at Carmarthen Bay, South Wales, write to the South Wales District of the CEGB, Crumlyn Burrows, Swansea.

Sewage works Many sewage works also have open days or welcome groups. Ring your regional water authority for details.

Index

Credits

The author and publishers would like to thank the following for their kind permission to reproduce copyright illustrations:

Aldus Archive/British
    Aerospace: 14
Angling Photo Service: 25
Barnaby's Picture Library: 5,
    7(bottom), 12-13, 20, 24, 34,
    40, 46-47, 51(top right, bottom
    right, bottom left)
British Tourist Authority: 51(top
    left)
Camerapix Hutchison Library:
    45
Earthscan/Mark Edwards: 22-23
Daily Telegraph Colour Library:
    cover
Farmers Weekly: 42
Ferranti Electronics Ltd: 7(top)
Greater London Council/
    Department of Public Health
    Engineering: 33
Sally and Richard Greenhill: 32,
    35, 58-59
Greenpeace: 28-29
The Guardian/Denis Thorpe: 17
Eric Hosking: 43
Mansell Collection: 18
NASA: 15
National Coal Board: 39
Naturfotografernas Bildbyra: 10
New Scientist: 30-31, 47
The Observer: 48-49
Popperfoto: 31, 52, 54-55, 56-57
Rex Features: 26-27
Homer Sykes: 37
Mireille Vautier: 19
Westfalisches Amt fur
    Denkmalpflege: 8, 9

Map page 36 by Norman Reynolds, from information supplied by *New Scientist*.

Picture research by Caroline Mitchell; design by Norman Reynolds.